Wild Hone

'In 1920, sixteen years after Chekh[...] unknown play by him came to light. The bulky manuscript, in Chekhov's own hand, was found inside a safe-deposit in a Moscow bank. The title page of the manuscript was missing, and with it all record of the play's identity and origins ... It is agreed by all authorities to be Chekhov's first extant play.'

So writes Michael Frayn in his detailed introduction to his brilliant new version of this mysterious play, which in the past has sometimes been called after its hero, Platonov. Frayn has taken a title from Chekhov's own text, which, he argues, 'evokes both the wayward sweetness of forbidden sexual attraction and the intense feeling of summer that pervades the play.'

Staged in full the original would run for some six hours, but, benefiting from his previous experience as translator of both *The Cherry Orchard* and *Three Sisters*, and as author of such plays as *Clouds, Make and Break* and *Noises Off*, Frayn has subtly cut and remodelled Chekhov's play while staying close to the spirit of the original. As he says, 'I have tried to recognise the story and characters that are beginning to emerge and to give them more definite dramatic form. I have tried to resolve the tone of the play by reducing the melodrama and by moving from lighter comedy at the beginning, through farce, to the darker and more painful comedy of the final scenes. The farcical element is not something I have imposed on the play; I have refocused it, but it was there in the original.'

The result is as if a little-known and delapidated painting had been restored to its pristine condition and revealed as a minor masterpiece to set in its rightful place beside the artist's other work. In fact, this *seventh* full-length Chekhov play is due to be given its first performances at the National Theatre, London, during 1984.

The photograph of Chekhov on the back cover is reproduced by courtesy of the Radio Times Hulton Picture Library.

Methuen's Theatre Classics

WILD HONEY

the untitled play by

Anton Chekhov

in a version by

Michael Frayn

METHUEN · LONDON AND NEW YORK

A METHUEN PAPERBACK

This version first published as a paperback original in 1984
by Methuen London Ltd, 11 New Fetter Lane, London EC4P 4EE
and Methuen Inc, 733 Third Avenue, New York, NY 10017, USA
Copyright in this version © 1984 by Michael Frayn
Introduction copyright © 1984 by Michael Frayn
Chronology copyright © 1978, 1983, 1984 by Michael Frayn

British Library Cataloguing in Publication Data

Frayn, Michael
    Wild honey — (Methuen's theatre classics)
    I Title II. Chekhov, A.P.
    822'.914   PR6056.R3

ISBN 0-413-55160-1

Set in IBM 10pt Journal by 🅰 Tek-Art, Croydon, Surrey
Printed in Great Britain by
Richard Clay (The Chaucer Press) Ltd,
Bungay, Suffolk

Anton Chekhov

1860 Born the son of a grocer and grandson of a serf, in Taganrog, a small port on the Sea of Azov, where he spends his first nineteen years, and which he describes on a return visit in later life as 'Asia, pure and simple!'

1875 His father, bankrupt, flees from Taganrog concealed beneath a mat at the bottom of a cart.

1876 A former lodger buys the Chekhovs' house and puts the rest of the family out.

1879 Chekhov rejoins his family, who have followed his father to Moscow, and enrols at the university to study medicine.

1880 Begins contributing humorous material to minor magazines under the pen-name Antosha Chekhonte.

1882 Begins contributing regularly to the St. Petersburg humorous journal *Oskolki* — short stories and sketches, and a column on Moscow life.

1884 Qualifies as a doctor, and begins practising in Moscow — the start of a sporadic career which over the years brings him much hard work but little income.

1885 Begins writing for the *St. Petersburg Gazette,* which gives him the opportunity to break out of the tight restrictions on length and the rigidly humorous format in which he has worked up to now.

1886 Another step up the journalistic ladder — he begins writing, under his own name and for good money, for *Novoye vremya.* Alexei Suvorin, its millionaire proprietor, an anti-Semitic reactionary who has the concession on all the railway bookstands in Russia, becomes Chekhov's close friend.

1887 Is a literary success in St. Petersburg. Writes *Ivanov* as a result of a commission from a producer who wants a light entertainment in the Chekhonte style. The play is produced in Moscow (his first production) to a mixture of clapping and hissing.

1888 Begins to publish his stories in the 'thick journals'; has survived his career in comic journalism to emerge as a serious and respectable writer. But at the same time begins writing four one-act farces for the theatre.

1889 *The Wood Demon* (which Chekhov later uses as raw material for *Uncle Vanya*) opens at a second-rate Moscow theatre, and survives for only three performances.

1890 Makes the appalling journey across Siberia (largely in unsprung carts over unsurfaced roads) to visit and report on the penal colony on the island of Sakhalin. Sets out to interview the entire population of prisoners and exiles, at the rate of 160 a day.

1892 Travels the back country of Nizhny Novgorod and Voronyezh provinces in the middle of winter, trying to prevent a recurrence of the previous year's famine among the peasants. Is banqueted by the provincial governors. Moves to the modest but comfortable estate he has bought himself at Melikhovo, fifty miles south of Moscow. Becomes an energetic and enlightened landowner, cultivating the soil and doctoring the peasants. Spends three months organizing the district against an expected cholera epidemic.

1894   Starts work on the first of the three schools he builds in the Melikhovo district.

1896   *The Seagull* opens in St. Petersburg, and survives only five performances after a disastrous first night. Chekhov tells Suvorin he won't have another play put on even if he lives another seven hundred years.

1897   Suffers a violent lung haemorrhage while dining with Suvorin, and is forced to recognize at last what he has long closed his eyes to — that he is suffering from advanced consumption. (Is also constantly plagued by piles, gastritis, migraine, dizzy spells, and palpitations of the heart.) Winters in Nice.

1898   Moves his headquarters to the Crimean warmth of Yalta. Stanislavsky revives *The Seagull* (with twelve weeks' rehearsal) at the newly-founded Moscow Arts Theatre, and it is an immediate success.

1899   Sells the copyright in all his works, past, present, and future, to the St. Petersburg publisher A.F. Marks — a contract which is to burden the rest of his life. *Uncle Vanya* produced successfully by the Moscow Arts Theatre.

1901   *Three Sisters* produced by the Moscow Arts Theatre, but rather poorly received. Chekhov marries hi mistress, Olga Knipper, an actress in the Moscow Arts company, who later creates the part of Ranyevskaya.

1904   *The Cherry Orchard* is produced in January; and in July, after two heart attacks, Chekhov dies in a hotel bedroom in the German spa of Badenweiler.

Introduction

In 1920, sixteen years after Chekhov's death, a new and unknown play by him came to light. The bulky manuscript, in Chekhov's own hand, was found inside a safe-deposit in a Moscow bank. The circumstances of the discovery are somewhat cloudy. But then there is an element of mystery about the play itself. The title-page of the manuscript was missing, and with it all record of the play's identity and origins. Since it was published by the Soviet Central State Literary Archive in 1923 it has become known under a variety of appellations. In England it is usually called by the name of its hero, Platonov; or rather, as English-speakers insist on pronouncing it, Plate On/Off. From the handwriting and the frequent provincial usages it was plainly written at the very beginning of Chekhov's career. In fact it is agreed by all authorities to be his first extant play. The puzzle is to know whether it is also the first full-length play that he ever wrote; and the question is not entirely academic.

It is a remarkable and tantalising work. Commentators seem to have been more struck by its youthful shortcomings than by its surprising strengths. Its defects are obvious enough. Its length, for a start; if it were staged uncut it would run, by my estimate, for something like six hours. In fact it is altogether too much. It has too many characters, too many disparate themes and aims, and too much action. It is trying to be simultaneously a sexual comedy, a moral tract, a melodrama, a state-of-Russia play, and a tragedy. The traces of Chekhov's early theatre-going as a school-boy in Taganrog (often in disguise, to elude the school inspector — it was a forbidden vice) are too baldly obvious. Platonov himself is that archetype of nineteenth-century Russian literature, the 'superfluous man'. He is also Hamlet, the hero crippled by conscience and indecision; and Chatsky (in Griboyedov's *Woe from Wit*), the hero incapacitated by chronic honesty. The play is also marred by a certain coarseness, particularly in the drawing of some of the minor characters; perhaps most particularly in the characterisation of Vengerovich, 'a wealthy Jew' (though his predictable vulgarity is somewhat counterbalanced by a streak of outspoken idealism in his son). Worse, for the workability of the play, is a rambling diffuseness of action and dialogue. Worse still, at any rate for the adaptor who is trying to find a practical solution to all these problems, is a defect that foreshadows one of the great glories of the later plays — a fundamental ambiguity of tone between comic and tragic, which will eventually be resolved into a characteristic Chekhovian mode, but which appears here mostly as an indeterminate wavering. All in all, it has been generally dismissed as unstageable. Ronald Hingley, in his biography, describes the play as a botched experiment which it is not surprising that Chekhov should have wished to bury in decent oblivion. What interests the commentators most is the way in which the later plays are here prefigured. Platonov is a sketch for Ivanov; Anna Petrovna, the widowed local landowner, foreshadows Ranyevskaya. There is the great theme of the lost estate, and the dispossession of the rural landowners by the new mercantile bourgeousie, that will recur in *The Cherry Orchard*. There is the unhappy wife attempting to poison herself, as in *Three Sisters*. There is the drunken doctor, and the vain longing of idle people to lose themselves in work, and so on.

All this is true. More striking by far, however, to someone engaged in the actual practice of playwriting, are the play's precocious and inimitable virtues. Platonov himself, for a start. He may be a mixture of Hamlet and Chatsky and others; but overwhelmingly, wonderfully, appallingly he is Platonov. He is not really like anyone else at all; he is not even remotely like his author. He is like himself, and — even more to the point — he just *is*. So is Anna Petrovna. She is a most surprising character to find in a nineteenth-century play. There are plenty of heroines of the time who inspire erotic feeling in men (and who usually end up dead or disfigured for their pains). There are a few, like Katerina Ismailovna in Leskov's *A Lady Macbeth of the Mtsensk District*, who are driven by some dark appetite of their own, and who pursue it to crime and degradation. But where else is there one who is permitted to express such shining physical desire, and to remain — though punished, it is true, by the loss of her estate —

essentially unhumiliated? And where else would such a powerful charge of feeling have led, by an only too human process of contrariness and confusion, to the seduction of the wrong woman? David Magarshack, in *Chekhov the Dramatist*, sees Anna Petrovna as a figure out of a mediaeval morality play, the personification of lust. She is nothing of the kind. She is a living, breathing, changeable human being who has a warm friendship for Platonov as well as desire. She repeatedly surprises — in the sudden impatience provoked by Platonov's vacillation, for example, and the sudden mean contempt with which she turns not only upon Sofya, when she discovers her to be her successful rival, but upon Sofya's wretched husband for failing to be man enough to control his wife; and perhaps most of all in the despair she reveals to Platonov in their last great scene together.

In this play for the first time we see Chekhov demonstrating his uncanny ability to enter the lives of people both unlike himself and outside his own experience. He makes Platonov 27, but the desperation that the reappearance of Sofya releases in him is the desperation of middle age, when we realise that our youth and promise have gone, and that we shall do no better in life. He does not specify Anna Petrovna's age; she is simply 'a young widow'. But she, too, is driven by the same fear that life is passing her by. It is difficult to understand how Chekhov could have known at the age he was then what it was like inside the hearts and minds of people who see their lives already beginning to slip from their grasp.

But what age *was* he exactly? This is where we come to the mystery. The only known account of the play's origin comes from Chekhov's younger brother Mikhail. He referred several times in articles and memoirs written in the years after Chekhov's death, to an 'unwieldy' play which he later specifically identified with the one found in the safe-deposit. He says that his brother wrote it 'in the year after his arrival in Moscow,' and 'in his second year at university' — both of which phrases fix the year as 1881, when Chekhov was 21, and studying medicine at Moscow University. (Chekhov's sister, in a letter written in the 1920s, refers to the play as having been written in his first year at university, which is not significantly different). Mikhail says that

Chekhov 'dreamed of having [it] produced at the Maly Theatre in Moscow,' and that he showed it to a well-known actress, M.N. Yermolova. In fact Mikhail says that he copied the play out for Chekhov, who took it round to Yermolova in person, in the hope that she would put it on for her benefit performance. And indeed on the first page of the manuscript from the safe-deposit (which is presumably the draft from which Mikhail worked when he copied it out) is a partly erased note in pencil, addressed to Marya Nikolayevna Yermolova saying: 'I am sending you . . . Mar Nik. Have no fear. Half of it is cut. In many places . . . still needs . . . Yours respectfully, A. Chekhov.' The actress was apparently not impressed. 'I do not know what answer Yermolova gave my brother,' wrote Mikhail later, 'but my efforts to make a legible copy of the drama went completely for nothing; the play was returned and was torn up by its author into little pieces.'

Now, this is puzzling enough. Chekhov, to judge by his other works, was not a precocious writer. At the age of twenty-one he had only just started out on his career as a humorous journalist, and the sketches and spoofs that he was producing then are short, facetious, and two-dimensional. They are often quite stylishly flippant, but they are within the range of a humorously-inclined medical student. The sheer size of the play would be surprising enough in this context. Donald Rayfield, in *Chekhov: the Evolution of his Art,* advances a plausible textual reason for dating the play two years later (a bizarre reference to Sacher-Masoch, whose works Rayfield believes Chekhov came across only when he was preparing his dissertation in 1883). But even then Chekhov had only just begun to write real stories. It is difficult to believe that he could have written some of the scenes in the play at that stage of his career. One might be tempted to suspect a forgery — except that it is even more difficult to believe that anyone else wrote them, at any stage in any career.

But this is only the beginning of the puzzle. Because two years before he entered university, when he was eighteen and still at school in Taganrog, Chekhov had already written a full-length drama. It was called *Bezotzovshchina,* and it was read both by his elder brother Alexander, who found in it two scenes of genius, but who dismissed the whole as unforgivable, and by Mikhail, who says he kept a copy of it until his brother arrived in Moscow to start university, when he asked for it back and tore it up into little pieces. This was the last anyone ever saw of it. Or was it? A play without a title, and a title without a play . . . Some scholars have always maintained that the two are in fact one.

On the face of it this is beyond belief. If it is difficult to imagine how Chekhov could have written the play when he was a medical student of 21, it is clearly even more difficult to imagine how he could have done it when he was a schoolboy of eighteen. Besides, if Mikhail was familiar with the first play, why should he say (as he does) that the play he copied out for Yermolova to read (and of which he lists details that plainly identify it with the one from the safe-deposit) was another one? It is possible to imagine that only one text was torn up into little pieces, and that Mikhail has attached one single recollection to two different occasions. It is very difficult to believe, though, that he would have failed to remark upon the fact if the play he had copied out was the same as the one he had seen before — or even noticeably similar to it.

Still, this was a quarter of a century and more after the events, and memory can be deceptive. It may be significant that in the final edition of his memoirs, in 1933, Mikhail expunged all reference to the destruction of either manuscript. And in the authoritative 30-volume *Complete Collected Works and Letters* of Chekhov which is now in the course of publication in Moscow, opinion has hardened in favour of the one-play theory. M.P. Gromov, in his exhaustive introduction to the play in this edition, bases his conclusions on the evidence of the handwriting and language; on the fact that none of the historical events referred to in the text occurred later than 1878; on the unlikelihood of Chekhov having in the course of four increasingly busy years written two major plays; on the provenance of the setting and some of the characters' names from the Taganrog area — there was for instance a General Platonov living next door to the school; and on the appropriateness of *Bezotzovshchina* as a title.

I am not competent to comment on the evidence of the

handwriting and language, and respect the intensive research on which Gromov has drawn. All the same, I am not sure that I find his arguments convincing enough to close the case. There is some evidence that he overlooks. He notes the date when Sacher-Masoch's book was translated into Russian (1877), but does not consider Rayfield's argument that Chekhov came across it only in 1883. Nor does he consider the many snatches of medical Latin in the text, or the plausibility of the symptoms in Platonov's attack of DTs, all of which suggest the medical student rather than the schoolboy.

Then again, *Bezotzovshchina,* which means the general condition of fatherlessness, seems to me to have no particular applicability to the play. This is why the question of the play's identity has some practical importance; if its title really is *Bezotzovshchina* then this plainly affects our reading of the text. Gromov argues that 'a desperate quarrel is occurring in the play between fathers and children . . . The children are insecure and unhappy because they do not have fathers whom they can respect.' In the original text, it is true, Platonov speaks bitterly about his memories of his drunken father, and this may reflect the feelings that Chekhov had about his own father's bullying mediocrity. But it has no real bearing upon the action of the play, and the other examples that Gromov offers of a 'quarrel' between the generations seem to me either insignificant or mis-construed, and in any case irrelevant to the action. No doubt everyone in the play would behave better if he had been better brought up; but then so would most of the characters in most of the world's plays.

Any reader with an interest in this, or in any of the other academic questions posed by the play, will have to consult the original text, which can be found in Volume 11 of the complete edition referred to above, or in Volume 12 of the more easily obtainable 20-volume edition by Yegolin and Tikhonov, published in 1948. There is also an English translation of the complete text by Ronald Hingley in Volume 2 of the Oxford Chekhov. The version that follows was commissioned by the National Theatre. It is not intended as an academic contribution or as a pious tribute, but as a text for production. It is extensively reworked, and I have not been influenced by Gromov's reading. There is no more reference to fatherlessness in what follows than there is to plates being turned on and off.

It is not, of course, the first time that this 'unstageable' play has been staged. It was done in England as *Platonov* at the Royal Court in 1960, with Rex Harrison playing the name part, in a fine translation by Dmitri Makaroff (who was once, briefly, one of my instructors in Russian). I follow with hesitation in the steps of one of my own teachers. But Makaroff's translation was simply a condensation of the original, and it seemed to me that it needed a more radical approach than this. Chekhov's text is more like a rough draft than a finished play. It may never have been intended as anything else. If Mikhail is right, Chekhov tore up the fair copy. The manuscript from the safe-deposit is quite heavily corrected already, but the pencilled note to Yermolova suggests that there were more corrections to come. Not that mere corrections would have been enough. Any translator of the late Chekhov plays becomes aware how tightly and elegantly organised they are — how each apparently casual and autonomous word is in fact advancing the business of the play. The more one works on these plays, the more exactly one wishes to recreate each line in English. But the more closely one looks at the text we are considering here, the more one's fingers itch to reshape it.

In fact the only way to proceed, it seemed to me, was to regard the play, if not the characters, as fatherless, and to adopt it — to treat it as if it were the rough draft of one of my own plays, and to do the best I could with it, whatever that involved. I have not sought to make it more like any of Chekhov's other plays. What I have tried to do is to recognise the story and characters that are beginning to emerge, and to give them more definite dramatic form. To this end I have felt free to reorganize the chronology of the play; to shift material from one place to another and one character to another; to write new lines and to rewrite old ones. I have cut out entire subplots. I have reduced the number of characters from twenty to sixteen, and brought on a couple more — two of the peasants who shoot Osip. I have tried to resolve the tone of the play by reducing the melodrama and the editorialising, and by moving from lighter comedy at the beginning, through farce, to the darker and more painful comedy of the final scenes. I should perhaps stress that the farcical element is not something that I have imposed upon the play. I have refocused it, but it was there in the original. So was the pervasive erotic atmosphere. So was the feminism. The emancipation of women was a topic of the time — Sofya refers to it in her first scene with Platonov. But the painful directness with which Anna Petrovna finally talks about her fate as an educated woman with nothing to do is something alive and felt — and it is there in the original, not added by me with hindsight as a nod to modern sensibilities.

Then there was the question of a title. The play has sometimes been called *Without Fathers*, from *Bezotzovshchina*, but I have explained my reasons for rejecting this. I am not enamoured of *Platonov* as a title, even if a national campaign could be launched to pronounce it correctly. It has also been called *That Worthless Fellow Platonov; Ce fou de Platonov;* and *Don Juan, in the Russian Manner.* They all suggest that the play centres exclusively around the one character, which is plainly not how Chekhov thought about it, or he would scarcely have offered it in the first place to an actress. The best title to date seems to me to be Alex Szogyi's *A Country Scandal.* But Chekhov himself has provided an even better one in the text. The play covers the period of the Voynitzevs' honeymoon (and its catastrophic end). Anna Petrovna refers to it in a phrase that seems to include all the various sexual intrigues — 'a month of wild honey' (in the original, 'a month smeared with wild honey'). This seems to me to evoke precisely both the wayward sweetness of forbidden sexual attraction, and the intense feeling of summer that pervades the play.

It is a presumptuous enterprise to rewrite someone else's work. I realise that by the very act of giving these characters and their story more definite form I have deprived them of the 'indefiniteness', the *neopredelyonnost'*, that Glagolyev in the original finds so pervasive in Russian society at the time, and of which he suggests Platonov as a hero; the very quality, so difficult to pin down precisely, that to a foreigner seems one of the most characteristically Russian at all times.

I was encouraged in my presumption, though, by a letter from Chekhov to his brother Alexander in 1882, urging him to approach the translations he was then doing with more freedom. 'Either don't translate rubbish, or do and polish it up as you go along. You can even cut and expand. The authors won't be offended, and you will acquire a reputation as a good translator.' The original in question here, of course, is far from being rubbish, and any virtues in what follows must be credited towards Chekhov's account, not mine.

One final puzzle – the circumstances of the play's discovery. This is a minor footnote to literary history. It has no bearing on our understanding of the play, but it does perhaps tell us a little more about Russian 'indefiniteness', and its survival in Soviet form.

In his otherwise scrupulously thorough introduction to the text in the new 30-volume Chekhov, Gromov becomes curiously evasive on the subject of the actual discovery. He merely quotes, without explanation, an account by N.F. Belchikov. Perhaps Nikolai Fyodorovich Belchikov, who died only recently, needs no introduction to Soviet readers. He was in fact the scholar who introduced and annotated the first edition of the play in 1923, after the fortunate discovery was made. He was thirty at the time, and he subsequently went on to a long and successful career as a Soviet literary specialist, joining the Party in 1948, at the height of Zhotanov's campaign against the arts, and ending up, in his late eighties, as head of the editorial board producing this same collected Chekhov in which Gromov is writing. Gromov quotes him thus: 'As N.F. Belchikov recounts, in the Moscow bank of the Russo-Azov Company were located the personal safes of its depositors. Here were preserved letters, documents, papers, little items of monetary or personal value, etc. Here among them was the safe of M.P. Chekhova. In it was discovered the manuscript of the play . . .'

Gromov does not say *where* Belchikov 'recounts' all this – an odd omission in such a scholarly edition. Perhaps it was over a glass of tea in the editorial offices. It was certainly not in Belchikov's own introduction to the first edition, where he says merely that the manuscript was among the Chekhov papers that 'were accessioned to the Central State Literary Archive in 1920' — a remarkably self-effacing formulation, because it is plain from Gromov's article that Belchikov was actually present when the great discovery was made. He says: 'N.F. Belchikov recalled, also lying in the same safe, an ancient stitched blue bead reticule that had possibly belonged to Y.Y. Chekhova [Chekhov's mother] .' In fact there is an odd air about the whole account, as quoted by Gromov — a *neopredelyonnost'* that seems characteristic of certain Soviet accounts of awkward events. It is a series of impersonal constructions that beg all the obvious questions about who opened the safe and why.

Now, a lot of human discovery is only relative. Columbus's discovery of America was no discovery to the Indians who lived there already. This discovery of the play, similarly, was scarcely a discovery to M.P. Chekhova, who had put the manuscript into her safe-deposit for the same reason that people usually put things into safe-deposits — precisely in order to stop them being 'discovered'. M.P. Chekhova was Chekhov's devoted sister Masha, who had inherited his house in Yalta, and all the papers inside it. From his death up to the time of the Revolution she had been hard at work sorting and publishing this material. In 1914, as Gromov himself mentions, she told the correspondent of the *Moscow Gazette* in Yalta: 'A long play without a title, written in the eighties, was recently found by me while sorting my brother's papers.'

So the discovery had already been discovered six years earlier. In a letter from Masha to Maxim Gorky written in 1918 she explains that she has moved all her brother's papers to Moscow for safekeeping — some of them to her flat in Dolgorukovskaya Street, 'the more precious' into a safe-deposit. Gromov does not mention this letter, written because Masha was desperately anxious about the fate of her brother's papers in Moscow during the period of the Revolution (she was unable to leave Yalta then because of her mother's illness) and wanted Gorky's help in having a guard put on both flat and safe-deposit until her arrival. But Gorky never received the letter, and in a note she appended later Masha recorded: 'And in the event AP's literary and other valuables were removed from the safe in my absence.'

Nor, curiously, does Gromov mention either of the other letters written by Masha that make clear her feelings about the 'discovery'. In 1921, after being cut off from Moscow for three years by the Civil War, she wrote to Meyerhold asking for his help in getting protection for her brother's papers; she had now heard that her flat in Dolgorukovskaya Street had been 'wrecked'. And in a letter to Nemirovich-Danchenko at the Moscow Arts Theatre, written a year or more later (the date is uncertain), she was still hoping that her brother's manuscripts, 'seized from me out of the safe-deposit, will in time be returned to me by the State Literary Archive.'

There is no reference, either, to the terrible journey that Masha undertook in 1921, as soon as it became possible to travel to Moscow, to find out what had happened to the papers. The Civil War had only just ended in the Crimea, and conditions were chaotic. The only place she could find in the overcrowded train was up in the luggage-rack, and she would have been put off *en route* as a class enemy if she had not happened to notice a boy reading one of Chekhov's stories in the compartment, and been able to identify herself as the writer's sister. She was 58 years old at the time. The journey took three weeks.

There may of course have been good reason why corners were cut, which Gromov felt his editor would be too modest to want publicised. All those indefinite impersonal constructions may conceal only the most diligent attempts to contact Masha in the war zone, and the most high-minded impatience to extend our knowledge of Chekhov's work. Belchikov's career would no doubt have prospered even without this windfall. In any case, what does it matter? Masha's safe-deposit was a very small egg among all the egggs that were broken to make that enormous omelette. She survived. In fact she was appointed official guardian of her brother's old house in Yalta, and lived to be 94. At the end of her life she wrote gratefully about how the new Soviet government had come to her aid in 1920. Perhaps there was a little tactful *neopredylonnost'* here, too. It hadn't seemed quite like that at the time, to judge by her letters, when the flat in Moscow was wrecked; when she got back from sorting that out only to find that the house in Yalta had been shot up by 'hooligan-bandits' in her absence, and she wrote to Nemirovich-Danchenko: 'At night I am alone in the whole house, I scarcely sleep, of course, I'm afraid and I don't know how I shall go on living. The prospect is a gloomy one — hunger, robbery, and the lack of any means of existence . . .! Please don't forget about me. Bear in mind that I am very afraid and that I am suffering. If there should happen to be any money to spare, please send me some — against royalties. I implore you!' nor when she added a wistful note about Nemirovich's life in the relative cleanliness of the Moscow Arts Theatre, where 'it smells of old times'; nor when she wrote to him again, some time between 1922 and 1924, complaining about the seizure of her brother's manuscripts from the safe-deposit, saying that 'there is among them much that is still unpublished, even a play written by him when he was a first-year student, all his letters to me, and up to some hundred photographs. A lot has disappeared, of course, such as relics, for example — I don't even want to remember it . . . I ought to come to Moscow myself and see to a great many things, but I am living in the most unfavourable conditions. My situation is undefined, unexplained, hopeless, and lonely. Many promises are made, but so far nothing has been done.'

Old and irrelevant pain. But perhaps worth recovering from the haze of the indefinite for one moment in all its sharpness.

Characters

The Voynitzev family

ANNA PETROVNA, *the late General Voynitzev's young widow*
VOYNITZEV, *Anna Petrovna's stepson, the general's son by his first marriage*
SOFYA, *Sergey's wife*
YAKOV ⎱
VASILY ⎰ *servants*

The Triletzky family

COLONEL TRILETZKY, *a retired artillery officer*
DOCTOR TRILETZKY, *the Colonel's son, the young local doctor*
SASHA, *the Colonel's daughter*
PLATONOV, *Sasha's husband, the local schoolmaster*

Other neighbours of the Voynitzevs'

GLAGOLYEV, *a local landowner*
PETRIN, *a wealthy merchant*
GREKOVA, *a young chemistry student*
OSIP, *the local horsethief, a man of thirty*
MARKO, *a little old man, process-server to the local Justice of the Peace*
TWO PEASANTS, *who are doubled with Yakov and Vasily*

The action takes place on the Voynitzev family estate in one of the southern provinces.

The Pronunciation of the Names

The following is an approximate practical guide. In general, all stressed a's are pronounced as in 'far' (the sound is indicated below by 'aa') and all stressed o's as in 'more' (they are written below as 'aw'). All unstressed a's and o's are thrown away and slurred. The u's are pronounced as in 'crude'; they are shown below as 'oo'.

Anna Petrovna Voynitzeva — *Aan*na Pe*trawv*na Vie-*neetz*eva

Sergey Pavlovich Voynitzev — Ser*gay Paav*lovich Vie-*neetz*ev

Sofya Yegorovna Voynitzeva — *Sawf*ya Ye*gawr*ovna Vie-*neetz*eva

Yakov — *Yaak*ov

Vasily — Va*seely*

Colonel Ivan Ivanovich Triletzky — Ee*vaan* Ee*vaan*ovich Tree*letz*ky

Doctor Nikolai Ivanovich Triletzky (Kolya) — Niko*lie* (as in 'lie' meaning 'untruth') Ee*vaan*ovich Tree*letz*ky (*Kawl*ya)

Alexandra Ivanovna Triletzkaya (Sasha, Sashenka) — Alek*sandr*a Ee*vaan*ovna Tree*letz*kaya (*Saash*a, *Saash*enka)

Mikhail Vasilyevich Platonov (Misha, Mishenka) — Meekha-*eel* Va*seely*evich Pla*tawn*ov (*Meesh*a, *Meesh*enka)

Porfiry Semyonovich Glagolyev — Por*feery* Sem*yawn*ovich Gla*gawl*yev

Gerasim Kuzmich Petrin (Gerasya) — Ge*raas*eem Kooz*meech* Pe*trin* (Ge*raas*ya)

Osip — *Aws*seep

Marko — *Maar*ko

Vova (the Platonovs' son) — *Vawv*a

Act One

Scene One

The drawing-room of the Voynitzevs' country house. Chairs, and a row of windows looking out on to a sunlit garden, with the tall trees of the forest beyond, bisected by a grassy walk.

The whoosh of a rocket taking off. The lights come up to reveal YAKOV *standing outside an open window with a large box of assorted fireworks in his arms. Beside him stands* DR TRILETZKY, *a match in his hand. They are gazing up into the sky —* DR TRILETZKY *with delight,* YAKOV *with apprehension. There is a smell of sulphur in the air. The rocket bursts off, and the stick falls into the garden.* YAKOV *backs away towards the house in alarm.* DR TRILETZKY *begins to light the touchpapers of all the rockets sticking up from the box.* YAKOV *backs away into the drawing-room.*

Enter ANNA PETROVNA *in alarm.*

ANNA PETROVNA. Doctor!

> YAKOV *turns to face* ANNA PETROVNA, *still holding the box of fireworks.*

DR TRILETZKY (*follows him in*); Fireworks!

ANNA PETROVNA (*to* YAKOV). Outside!

YAKOV. Outside . . . (*He puts the fireworks down and flees.*)

ANNA PETROVNA. Yakov! Come back! Take the fireworks!

> YAKOV *picks them up uncertainly.*

Now, outside! Quick! Run!

> *Exit* YAKOV *hurriedly with the box.*

(*To* DR TRILETZKY.) For heaven's sake! They'll all go up! The whole house will be in flames!

> *The sound of a series of rockets departing, off.*

ANNA PETROVNA. Doctor, really! They're for later! When it gets dark!

DR TRILETZKY. Anna Petrovna! (*He takes her hand.*) It's all your fault! (*He kisses her hand.*)

ANNA PETROVA. *My* fault?

> *Enter* YAKOV, *with the blackened box of fireworks, and a blackened face.*

(*To* YAKOV:) Take them away! Behind the old summerhouse! I told you before.

> *Exit* YAKOV *through the garden.*

My fault?

DR TRILETZKY. Of course! You're back! So we're all quite light-headed. You don't know what it's been like here in the country without you. I can't imagine how we've all survived the winter. Was it wonderful in town? Did you go to the theatre? Did you have dinner in restaurants? Did you miss us all? Are you pleased to be back? Or are you bored already? If you think this place is dull when you're here you should be here when you're *not* here. We all live under dust-covers, like the furniture. But now you're back, and the covers are off, and it's the first perfect day of summer, and when are we going to eat?

ANNA PETROVNA. Not for ages yet. Cook's got drunk to celebrate our arrival . . . Are you feeling my pulse, doctor? Or are you taking a little bite to keep you going until lunchtime?

DR TRILETZKY. I was just thinking. You arrived last night?

ANNA PETROVNA. On the evening train.

DR TRILETZKY. Where did you get the fireworks, then?

ANNA PETROVNA. Your father sent them. He came over first thing this morning.

DR TRILETZKY. He's shameless! He could have waited until lunch, like the rest of us. He is coming to lunch?

ANNA PETROVNA. Of course. We must have the colonel.

DR TRILETZKY. And Porfiry Semyonovich is here already. I met him in the garden with your stepson.

ANNA PETROVNA. Poor Sergey! But I endured him for an hour or more first.

DR TRILETZKY. So you'll have us all at your feet again. Just like last summer.

GLAGOLYEV *appears in the garden, making frequent halts to lean on his stick and pontificate to* VOYNITZEV, *who listens with perfect deference.*

ANNA PETROVNA. Here comes Porfiry Semyonovich now.

DR TRILETZKY. He was telling Sergey about the decline in modern manners when I met them.

ANNA PETROVNA. What a cruel stepmother I am!

GLAGOLYEV (*to* VOYNITZEV): No, we had real respect for them, you see.

VOYNITZEV. Like the knights of old.

GLAGOLYEV. We looked up to them.

VOYNITZEV. You put them on a pedestal.

GLAGOLYEV. We put them on a pedestal.

DR TRILETZKY. I think they've got on to the subject of women.

GLAGOLYEV. We loved women, certainly. But we loved them in the way that the knights of old loved them.

VOYNITZEV. You had respect for them.

GLAGOLYEV. We had respect for them.

DR TRILETZKY. Your stepson has become the most agreeable of men.

ANNA PETROVNA. Poor Sergey!

DR TRILETZKY. He goes away an artist and poet. He comes back with his beard shaved off — and underneath he's not an artist and poet at all! He's a very agreeable young man like everybody else.

ANNA PETROVNA. He doesn't need an artistic nature now. He has a wife instead.

GLAGOLYEV (*to* VOYNITZEV): So you see, we poor old setting stars have the advantage of you young rising stars!

VOYNITZEV. You knew the world when the world was young.

DR TRILETZKY. All your old admirers! However will you bear it? Where's Platonov? You'll never put up with us all without Platonov here to amuse you.

ANNA PETROVNA. I've sent across for him twice already.

> GLAGOLYEV *and* VOYNITZEV *approach the drawing-room.*

GLAGOLYEV (*to* VOYNITZEV): No, we believed in women, we worshipped the ground they walked on, because we saw in woman the better part of man . . .

DR TRILETZKY. I'll tell Vasily to run over there again.

> *Exit* DR TRILETZKY.

> GLAGOLYEV *and* VOYNITZEV *come in from the garden.*

GLAGOLYEV. Anna Petrovna! We were just talking about the fair sex, as chance would have it.

ANNA PETROVNA. You have always given the subject a great deal of time and attention.

GLAGOLYEV. I was saying to your stepson that woman is the better part of man. Or so we believed in my day. So your late husband believed, I know that, God rest his soul. (*To* VOYNITZEV.) Oh yes, your father was like me, God give him peace — one of the old school . . . So hot! I must sit down, I'm quite done up . . .

ANNA PETROVNA. You had your friends, too, of course.

GLAGOLYEV. We had our friends, too. The general had his friends. (*To* VOYNITZEV.) Your father had a wide circle of friends.

VOYNITZEV. And friendship in your day was not the here-today-gone-tomorrow thing it is now.

GLAGOLYEV. We were ready to go through the fire for our friends.

VOYNITZEV. The only people who'll go through the fire for anyone these days are firemen.

GLAGOLYEV. Firemen?

ANNA PETROVNA. Sergey!

VOYNITZEV. Sorry. My mind was wandering.

GLAGOLYEV (*to* VOYNITZEV): No, we were happier than you. You never knew the past. You'd sing a different tune if you had!

> COLONEL TRILETZKY *appears in the garden, leaning on a stick like* GLAGOLYEV.

VOYNITZEV. And here's the colonel.

GLAGOLYEV. The colonel, was it, who sent those fireworks?

ANNA PETROVNA. The colonel is always ready to go through the fireworks for his friends.

GLAGOLYEV. Dangerous things, fireworks. I'm no great lover of fireworks.

> COLONEL TRILETZKY *comes in from the garden.*

COLONEL TRILETZKY (*to* ANNA PETROVNA): Your Majesty!

ANNA PETROVNA. Colonel!

COLONEL TRILETZKY. A twenty-one gun salute to the queen of the district! (*He raises the stick into his shoulder.*) Bang bang bang! Bang bang . . . !

VOYNITZEV. Colonel! Still ready with a salvo?

COLONEL TRILETZKY. Sergey Pavlovich!

VOYNITZEV. You're well, are you?

COLONEL TRILETZKY. I'm always well. The good Lord endures

me with remarkable patience. Porfiry Semyonovich!

GLAGOLYEV (*disgusted*): Fireworks!

COLONEL TRILETZKY (*to* ANNA PETROVNA): Arrived, have they?

ANNA PETROVNA. So kind of you. Something for us all to look forward to.

COLONEL TRILETZKY. Only supporting fire I can provide these days.

GLAGOLYEV. He'll blow you all up if you're not careful.

COLONEL TRILETZKY. A twenty-one rocket salute! (*He raises the stick into his shoulder.*)

    Enter DR TRILETZKY.

DR TRILETZKY. Don't shoot! It's your long-lost son!

COLONEL TRILETZKY. Kolya!

DR TRILETZKY. And in the nick of time, by the look of it.

COLONEL TRILETZKY (*lowers his stick, and embraces* DR TRILETZKY *with emotion*): My dear boy!

DR TRILETZKY. Father!

COLONEL TRILETZKY. Haven't seen you for . . . what . . .?

DR TRILETZKY. It must be nearly two weeks now, Father.

COLONEL TRILETZKY. Have to come to Anna Petrovna's to see my own son! Keep meaning to call on you. Never manage it. Too busy! Going to come over yesterday. Show you my new twelve-bore. Stopped by the police, though! Got caught to play cards with the Superintendent. (*To* ANNA PETROVNA.) Wonderful gun. Bring it over and show you. Double-barrelled. English. Fill you full of shot at 200 paces.

DR TRILETZKY (*to* ANNA PETROVNA): Summer again, and your little court is assembling for the season.

ANNA PETROVNA. It's not me you've all come to see this time. It's my new daughter-in-law.

DR TRILETZKY (*to* VOYNITZEV): Yes! Where is she?

COLONEL TRILETZKY. Of course! He's got married! There's my memory for you!

ANNA PETROVNA (*to* VOYNITZEV): Everyone's longing to meet her.

COLONEL TRILETZKY. But what a funny fellow! Gets married, and never says a word about it! Talks about nothing but guns! Well, life and happiness to you, Sergey Pavlovich! Life and happiness! Is she beautiful?

ANNA PETROVNA. Enchanting!

COLONEL TRILETZKY. Two queens on the board against us! We're done for!

DR TRILETZKY. Fetch her out, then! It's not fair to keep us all in suspense.

ANNA PETROVNA. Especially Porfiry Semyonovich. He's such a great lover of women.

GLAGOLYEV. I certainly prefer them to sporting guns and fireworks.

VOYNITZEV. I think she's walking under the trees. I'll see if I can find her.

VOYNITZEV *goes out into the garden.*

COLONEL TRILETZKY (*takes* ANNA PETROVNA's *hand*). This is the girl for me, though!

ANNA PETROVNA (*to* DR TRILETZKY). Your father's going to take me quail-shooting.

GLAGOLYEV. If you are interested in birds, I could show you several quite rare species on my estate.

DR TRILETZKY (*to* ANNA PETROVNA): They're fighting over you!

ANNA PETROVNA (*a hand on both their arms*): We'll all come and see your birds. We'll bring the colonel's new twelve-bore.

COLONEL TRILETZKY. God strike me down, but this is the girl for me! The emancipation of women in person, this one! Get a sniff of her shoulder! Powder! A warrior-chief, if ever I saw one! Put a pair of epaulettes on her and she'd outgeneral the lot of us!

GLAGOLYEV. Have you been drinking already, colonel?

COLONEL TRILETZKY. Of course I have! Started at eight o'clock this morning! Came over here — found everyone asleep apart from the empress herself. Couldn't have been more delighted to see me, so we split a bottle of Madeira.

ANNA PETROVNA. You didn't have to tell everyone!

GLAGOLYEV. When you come to visit me we shall sample a glass of my housekeeper's whortleberry liqueur.

Enter VOYNITZEV *and* SOFYA *through the garden.*

DR TRILETZKY. And here she is!

VOYNITZEV *stops to present* SOFYA *with a flower. They laugh together.*

COLONEL TRILETZKY. Oh, but she's an absolute bullseye!

ANNA PETROVNA. I told you!

GLAGOLYEV. Charming couple.

DR TRILETZKY. The ideal stepson.

ANNA PETROVNA. And the ideal wife for him.

VOYNITZEV *and* SOFYA *come in from the garden.*

SOFYA. Oh, Anna Petrovna, I've never seen such a beautiful garden! I'm quite dizzy with sunlight and the scent of flowers! And I've been walking in the forest. It's so cool under the trees, and there's a kind of faint sound in the air all the time, as if the forest were sighing to itself with pure happiness. I can't imagine living in such a place.

ANNA PETROVNA. Well, now you do, my dear.

SOFYA. Do I really?

VOYNITZEV. It's all yours.

SOFYA. It's like a dream! I'm afraid I shall reach out to touch it and everything will vanish.

COLONEL TRILETZKY. Aren't you going to introduce us?

ANNA PETROVNA. Oh, yes, now, Sofya, these are your new neighbours. The colonel . . .

COLONEL TRILETZKY Triletzky. Ivan Ivanovich.

ANNA PETROVNA. Who will take you duck-shooting at dawn . . .

COLONEL TRILETZKY. Snipe! That mighty swamp on Porfiry Semyonovich's estate must be full of them! A great polar expedition! We'll all go!

ANNA PETROVNA. Sofya Yegorovna. And this is the colonel's son . . .

DR TRILETZKY. Nikolai Ivanovich.

ANNA PETROVNA. He's the local doctor, who will nurse you back to health again afterwards. And this is Porfiry Semyonovich, the owner of the mighty swamp. He is . . . what are you, Porfiry Semyonovich? He is a great lover of women.

SOFYA. Really?

GLAGOLYEV. I make the claim in all humility.

SOFYA. And Platonov. Isn't he here?

VOYNITZEV. Yes — Sofya knows Platonov!

SOFYA. Only slightly.

VOYNITZEV. But isn't that extraordinary?

SOFYA. I don't suppose he'll know me.

DR TRILETZKY. Of course he will! Platonov knows everything.

COLONEL TRILETZKY. He certainly knows all the pretty women!

GLAGOLYEV. Really, colonel! We're talking about a serious scholar!

COLONEL TRILETZKY. Our local Socrates!

ANNA PETROVNA (*to* DR TRILETZKY): Where is he?

DR TRILETZKY. I sent Vasily running.

SOFYA. He was a student when I met him. I was only a schoolgirl. He won't remember me.

VOYNITZEV. We'll see! We won't introduce you. We'll find
out what kind of scholar he really is!

SOFYA. Oh, but it's so lovely here!

    Enter VASILY.

DR TRILETZKY. The perfect picture of country life! We're
only missing one thing . . .

ANNA PETROVNA. Yes, is he coming Vasily?

VASILY. Directly, he says, Anna Petrovna, but Anna Petrovna,
it's Marko.

ANNA PETROVNA. Marko?

VASILY. From the magistrate, Anna Petrovna.

ANNA PETROVNA. Marko the process-server?

DR TRILETZKY. What, with a summons?

VASILY. Big envelope, it is.

VOYNITZEV (*to* ANNA PETROVNA). He's done it!

ANNA PETROVNA. Of course he hasn't. Not on our first day
back.

SOFYA. Done what?

ANNA PETROVNA. Nothing.

VOYNITZEV. He's taken us to court! He's suing us on the
bills!

SOFYA. Who is?

ANNA PETROVNA. No one.

VOYNITZEV. We've lost the estate!

ANNA PETROVNA. Don't be ridiculous. It's all some silly mistake. (*To* VASILY:) Send the man in.

VASILY. This way . . .

> *Enter* MARKO, *an old man with a neat, soldierly bearing. He has an envelope in his hands, and more envelopes in a satchel round his neck.*

DR TRILETZKY (*to* SOFYA): The old general was sick.

MARKO. Anna Petrovna Voynitzeva?

COLONEL TRILETZKY (*to* SOFYA): He signed anything they put in front of him.

ANNA PETROVNA. Give it to me, then.

> MARKO *hands her the envelope.*

I'll open it later.

VOYNITZEV (*to* MARKO): Yes, you come bursting in here, badgering my stepmother in front of her guests . . .

MARKO. Sergey Pavlovich Voynitzev?

VOYNITZEV. Yes?

> MARKO *hands him another envelope. He gazes at it in astonishment.*

DR TRILETZKY. Sergey! What have you been up to?

MARKO. Dr Nikolai Ivanovich Triletzky?

DR TRILETZKY. Me?

> MARKO *hands him an envelope. He gazes at it in astonishment in his turn.*

ANNA PETROVNA. You, too?

GLAGOLYEV. My dear Anna Petrovna, if you will allow me to be of assistance . . .

MARKO. Porfiry Semyonovich Glagolyev?

GLAGOLYEV. I beg your pardon?

ANNA PETROVNA. Not you!

MARKO *hands him an envelope. He gazes at it, flabber-gasted. They all look at each other's envelopes.*

What, have we all got one, then?

COLONEL TRILETZKY. Not me! Wouldn't do it to an old soldier! Old soldier yourself, aren't you?

MARKO. Artillery, sir.

COLONEL TRILETZKY. Thought so! Corporal Marko, wasn't it? Nikolaevsky Regiment?

MARKO. That's it, sir. And you're Colonel Triletzky?

COLONEL TRILETZKY. That's right!

MARKO. Colonel Ivan Ivanovich Triletzky?

COLONEL TRILETZKY. Exactly!

MARKO *hands him an envelope.*

Not a man left standing!

ANNA PETROVNA. Look at Sofya staring.

SOFYA. No, no!

ANNA PETROVNA. I suppose we'd better open them.

They open them.
GREKOVA *appears in the garden. She stops, awkward and flustered, to dab a handkerchief to her face.*

DR TRILETZKY *is the only one to notice her.*

DR TRILETZKY (*goes to meet her*). Marya Yefimovna!

ANNA PETROVNA (*reads*): 'His Imperial Majesty's Justice of the Peace . . .'

VOYNITZEV (*reads*): '. . . will be at home on Sunday June the fifteenth . . .'

GLAGOLYEV (*reads*):' . . . on the occasion of his son's christening . . .'

ANNA PETROVNA. It's not a summons!

MARKO. No, ma'am.

COLONEL TRILETZKY. It's an invitation!

MARKO. Yes, sir.

DR TRILETZKY (*brings* GREKOVA *into the room*): It's Marya Yefimovna . . .

> *The others look up from their letters, and burst out laughing with relief.* GREKOVA *takes one horrified look at them, and flees back into the garden.*

ANNA PETROVNA. Oh dear. What an unfortunate moment to choose!

DR TRILETZKY (*embarrassed*): I think she's just looking in by chance . . . I happened to mention that you would be back today . . .

VOYNITZEV. No, it's a christening, you see! That's what we're summoned to!

ANNA PETROVNA. Poor Sofya! She must have wondered what kind of family she'd come into!

SOFYA. No, but I think that other poor girl must have wondered a little.

ANNA PETROVNA. Oh, yes, poor Marya Yefimovna! She comes seven miles on a hot afternoon, and what happens?

COLONEL TRILETZKY. She gets her head blown off! Same thing every time she comes here. Walks in — head blown off.

VOYNITZEV. It's usually Platonov who does it.

ANNA PETROVNA. He's not even here, and already she's hiding under the trees again. It's just like last year.

COLONEL TRILETZKY. Never get her back now.

DR TRILETZKY (*looking at his letter*): A christening . . . I suppose I should try . . .

SOFYA. I'll go. I know what it's like, coming into a room full of people.

> SOFYA *goes out into the garden, followed by* VOYNITZEV.

GLAGOLYEV. Charming young woman!

ANNA PETROVNA. Go and help her, Porfiry Semyonovich.

COLONEL TRILETZKY. We'll all go and help her! (*To* MARKO.) And we'll all come to the christening on Sunday! Sevastopol?

MARKO. And Balaclava, sir.

COLONEL TRILETZKY. See it in your eyes. (*He gives him a coin.*)

MARKO. Thank you, sir.

> GLAGOLYEV *and* COLONEL TRILETZKY *go into the garden.*

DR TRILETZKY. I'd better go and talk to her.

ANNA PETROVNA. I think you'd better stay and talk to me. (*To* VASILY:) Take him out to the kitchen and give him something to drink. Fancy telling us he was bringing a summons!

> *Exeunt* VASILY *and* MARKO.

So! It wasn't me you came to see at all!

DR TRILETZKY. Anna Petrovna, I was sure she wouldn't come! I thought she'd refused to set foot in the same house as Platonov again, after all that business last summer.

ANNA PETROVNA. I like her! I love her sharp little nose. Is she still studying chemistry?

DR TRILETZKY. She reads books, too.

> *They watch her out of the window.* COLONEL TRILETZKY *and* GLAGOLYEV *approach her, but are taken discreetly aside by* VOYNITZEV, *leaving* SOFYA *to stroll with her under the trees.*

ANNA PETROVNA. Are you serious about her?

DR TRILETZKY. Platonov thinks she's a fool. That's what the trouble was last summer. He's got it into that unkempt head of his that he has some kind of mission in life to rebuke fools.

ANNA PETROVNA. I know what a fool *you* are. Plenty of brains in that head of yours, but they're not always much in evidence. *Are* you serious?

DR TRILETZKY. I call on her nearly every day. I make conversation, I endure the boredom, I put her poor mother to some expense in coffee, and there we are. I talk about what interests me; she talks about what interests her. Then she takes hold of me by the lapels, and brushes the dust off my collar. I always seem to be covered in dust. But quite what draws me back each time, whether it's love or whether it's boredom, I don't really know.

Pause. SOFYA *and* GREKOVA *disappear among the trees.*

ANNA PETROVNA. Silence. Somewhere a fool was being born.

DR TRILETZKY. All I know is that I miss her quite painfully after lunch sometimes.

ANNA PETROVNA. So it's love, then. And here he is.

PLATONOV *and* SASHA *appear in the garden.*

VOYNITZEV. Platonov!

COLONEL TRILETZKY. Mishenka! My dear fellow!

PLATONOV. Sergey Pavlovich!

Joyful kisses and handclasps are exchanged.

VOYNITZEV. You've put on weight!

PLATONOV. You've taken off your beard!

VOYNITZEV (*to* SASHA): Alexandra Ivanovna!

PLATONOV (*shakes hands with* GLAGOLYEV): Porfiry Semyo-novich.

GLAGOLYEV. We've been talking about you, Platonov.

COLONEL TRILETZKY. Late on parade again!

PLATONOV. Colonel!

COLONEL TRILETZKY. Keeping Her Majesty waiting!

ANNA PETROVNA (*to* DR TRILETZKY): Now we shall be all right.

> VOYNITZEV, COLONEL TRILETZKY *and* GLAGOLYEV *escort* PLATONOV *and* SASHA *into the house in triumph.*

PLATONOV. At last — we're away from home! Anna Petrovna . . . !

VOYNITZEV. Here he is!

COLONEL TRILETZKY. This is the man!

PLATONOV. Say hello to everyone, Sasha . . . Anna Petrovna! (*He takes both her hands and kisses them.*)

ANNA PETROVNA. Cruel man! How could you make us wait so long? You must have known how impatient I should be. Alexandra Ivanovna! My dear! (*She kisses* SASHA.)

PLATONOV. Out of our house at last! Glory be to God! We haven't seen high ceilings for six whole months! We haven't seen people! We've been hibernating in our lair like two old bears, and we've only crawled forth into the world today!

VOYNITZEV. But you have — you've put on weight! Hasn't he! You've got larger! And Alexandra Ivanovna! What can I say . . . ? Are you well?

PLATONOV. She's fine, she's fine. And her ladyship's household physician is in attendance, I see. (*He embraces* DR TRILETZKY.) Radiant with health, by the look of it. Drenched in perfume, by the smell of it.

DR TRILETZKY (*kisses* SASHA): It's true — he has put on weight. He's as big as a bull in a china shop.

PLATONOV. And that haircut must have cost you a ruble or two.

DR TRILETZKY. You should be pleased to have a well turned-out brother-in-law.

ANNA PETROVNA. But how are you both? Sit down! Tell us everything! We'll all sit down.

PLATONOV (*to* VOYNITZEV, *laughing*): Is this really you?

Heavens above! Where's the beard and the long hair? Even the voice has changed! Come on — let's hear you say something!

VOYNITZEV. I feel a complete fool!

PLATONOV. He's a bass! He's an absolute basso profundo! What happened to that charming light tenor you used to have?

SASHA. Sergey Pavlovich, I must just say one thing . . .

PLATONOV. Sasha, my love, will you never stop talking?

SASHA (*to* VOYNITZEV): Congratulations.

PLATONOV. Oh, yes! Of course!

SASHA. May I wish you every possible happiness?

PLATONOV. You've got yourself married! My warmest congratulations, too! (*He bows.*) Love and harmony all your days! Who is the lady?

VOYNITZEV. You'll see.

PLATONOV. I must confess I never expected it of you. Rather an about-face for a man of your views.

VOYNITZEV. Well, you know me. Always quick off the mark! Fell in love — married her!

PLATONOV. We've had the falling in love part every winter. It's the getting married that's such a novel departure. Have you found a job?

VOYNITZEV. I've been offered a job in a high school of sorts, and I don't know what to do. It's not what I should have chosen.

PLATONOV. You'll take it, though?

VOYNITZEV. I really don't know. Probably not.

PLATONOV. So you'll be letting more time slip by. Three years now, isn't it, since you left university? You need someone to give you a bit of a kick. I must have a word with your wife. Three good years wasted! Isn't that right?

DR TRILETZKY. He hasn't been in the house five minutes, and

already he's flaying us all!

GLAGOLYEV. Well, it's rare enough these days — someone with clear moral standards.

COLONEL TRILETZKY. My own son-in-law — the village Savonarola!

ANNA PETROVNA (*to* PLATONOV): Yes, go on! How have we got through the winter without your moral refreshment?

PLATONOV. It's too hot today to be serious. And it's far too pleasant sitting here again to be indignant at the evils of the world . . . I can see Sasha positively sniffing the air.

SASHA. Yes, I was. (*He laughs.*)

PLATONOV. You know what it smells of here? Human flesh! And what a delightful smell it is! I feel as if we hadn't seen each other for a hundred years. The winter went on and on forever! And there's my old armchair! Recognise it, Sasha? Six months ago I was never out of it. Sat there day and night talking to Anna Petrovna about the nature of the world, and losing all the housekeeping at cards.

ANNA PETROVNA. I've been so longing to see you again! I was quite out of patience . . . And you're well?

PLATONOV. Very well . . . But I must tell you one piece of news: you have grown just a shade more beautiful than before.

ANNA PETROVNA. And you've both put on weight! Such lucky people! So how have things been?

PLATONOV. Terrible, as usual. Never saw the sky for the whole six months. Ate, drank, slept. And read schoolboy adventure stories aloud to my wife. Terrible!

ANNA PETROVNA (*to* SASHA): Was it?

SASHA. I thought it was lovely.

PLATONOV. Sasha, it was appalling!

SASHA. It was a little bit dull, naturally.

PLATONOV. It wasn't a little bit dull, my love — it was extremely dull. (*To* ANNA PETROVNA:) I was pining for you!

SASHA. You got back yesterday?

ANNA PETROVNA. On the evening train.

PLATONOV. I saw lights here at eleven, but I thought you would be tired out.

ANNA PETROVNA. You should have come in! We sat up talking until two.

PLATONOV. So hot today. And so oppressive.

GLAGOLYEV. I think we may have a storm.

PLATONOV. I'm already starting to pine for the cold again.

COLONEL TRILETZKY. Sashenka, Sashenka! (*He puts a hand on* SASHA's *arm.*)

DR TRILETZKY. I thought you were asleep.

COLONEL TRILETZKY. My daughter . . . my son-in-law . . . my son . . All the great stars of the Colonel Triletzky constellation! (*To* SASHA:) Always meaning to call on you. See my grandson. Set the world to rights with Mishenka here. Never manage to call on anyone, though. Too busy, you see, my love! Have to wait for Her Majesty to bring us all together. Strange . . .

DR TRILETZKY. If we're not careful he's going to be weeping at the sight of us all. Aren't you, Father.

COLONEL TRILETZKY. Weep? Why should I want to weep?

DR TRILETZKY. Because you always do! Look at us all! What a family! And think of your grandson!

COLONEL TRILETZKY (*to* SASHA): Yes, how is the little fellow? Come and see him one of these days.

SASHA. He's well. He sends you his love.

COLONEL TRILETZKY. Really? Amazing child he is! Knows how to send his love to people now, does he?

VOYNITZEV. I think she means metaphorically speaking, colonel.

PLATONOV. He's not one yet, Father-in-law!

DR TRILETZKY. No, he's always talking about you! He waves his little arms and he pipes: 'Grandpapa! Grandpapa! Where's my grandpapa?'

PLATONOV. He's eleven months old!

DR TRILETZKY. 'I want to pull my grandpapa's moustache!'

COLONEL TRILETZKY. Good for him! (*He takes out his hand-kerchief.*) But you're not going to get me crying about it!

DR TRILETZKY. I don't see tears, do I, colonel?

PLATONOV. Stop it now, Kolya.

DR TRILETZKY. All right, so how about Anna Petrovna feeding us instead?

ANNA PETROVNA. You'll have to wait, doctor, like everybody else.

DR TRILETZKY. She doesn't realise how hungry we are. It's all on the table in there! Caviar, salmon, smoked sturgeon. A great seven-storey pie . . .

ANNA PETROVNA. How do you know what there is?

DR TRILETZKY. I went in and looked! Aren't you hungry, Porfiry Semyonovich? Be absolutely frank, now!

SASHA (*to* DR TRILETZKY): You're not all that hungry — you just want to make trouble. You can't bear to see people sitting there in peace.

DR TRILETZKY. I can't bear to see people dying of hunger, Fat Lady.

PLATONOV. Another flash of quicksilver medical wit.

ANNA PETROVNA. What a bore the man is! All right, impudence, you wait here and I'll find you something to eat.

Exit ANNA PETROVNA.

PLATONOV. Though it wouldn't come amiss, now you mention it. I'm rather hungry myself.

SOFYA *and* GREKOVA *appear in the garden.*

VOYNITZEV. Here are the ladies, anyway. Now we'll put our great scholar to the test!

PLATONOV. Who is it?

VOYNITZEV. Aha!

COLONEL TRILETZKY. She's coaxed our little bolter back, by the look of it. (*To* PLATONOV:) Took one look at us before and fled!

PLATONOV. Who are we talking about?

DR TRILETZKY. Oh, yes, and now you're here!

COLONEL TRILETZKY. Come in and go straight out again, I should think!

GLAGOLYEV. May I suggest we pay her no attention?

VOYNITZEV. Just concentrate on the other one, Platonov, and tell us who she is.

SOFYA *ushers* GREKOVA *in from the garden.*

PLATONOV. Oh, it's the beetle-juice girl!

GREKOVA *stops in her tracks.*
PLATONOV *pays no attention to* SOFYA, *who watches the scene gravely.*

DR TRILETZKY (*reproachfully*). Misha!

GREKOVA (*coldly*). Mikhail Vasilyevich.

PLATONOV (*takes her hand*). Marya Yefimovna! My compliments!

VOYNITZEV. And here is someone else who is longing to meet you, Platonov . . .

PLATONOV. One moment. It's such a pleasure to meet Marya Yefimovna again. (*He tries to kiss her hand.*)

GREKOVA (*pulls her hand back*). I don't want my hand kissed. Thank you.

PLATONOV. I'm not worthy to kiss your hand, even?

GREKOVA. I've no idea whether you're worthy or not. I just know you don't mean it.

PLATONOV. Don't mean it? What makes you think that?

GREKOVA. You know I don't like it. That's the only reason you do it. It's always the same — you only like doing things that I don't like you doing.

DR TRILETZKY. Leave her alone, Misha.

PLATONOV. All in good time. (*To* GREKOVA:) How are you progressing with your beetle-juice?

GREKOVA. Beetle-juice? What is this about beetle-juice?

PLATONOV. Someone told me you were trying to make ether out of crushed beetles. Pushing forward the boundaries of science. Admirable!

GREKOVA. You must always make a joke of everything, mustn't you.

DR TRILETZKY. Always! Of everything!

PLATONOV. I make the doctor my model.

VOYNITZEV. Platonov . . .

PLATONOV. But what a charming pink your cheeks are! You're feeling the heat, I can see.

GREKOVA. Why do you keep saying these things to me?

PLATONOV. I'm merely trying to hold a conversation with you. I haven't talked to you for six months or more. Why are you getting so cross about it?

GREKOVA. The sight of me seems to have some strange effect on you. I don't know how I've managed to upset you so. I stay out of your way as far as I possibly can. If Dr Triletzky hadn't promised me faithfully that you wouldn't be here I shouldn't have come.

DR TRILETZKY. I said I didn't know whether he'd be here or not.

GREKOVA (*to* DR TRILETZKY): You should be ashamed of yourself!

PLATONOV (*to* DR TRILETZKY): Absolutely! Deceiving her like that! (*To* GREKOVA:) Now you're going to cry, aren't you. All right — have a little cry, then. It can sometimes be a great relief.

Exit GREKOVA *in tears.*

DR TRILETZKY (*to* PLATONOV): You're such an idiot! One more little incident of that sort and we'll never be friends again!

PLATONOV. What's it to do with you?

DR TRILETZKY. Well, let's suppose — just for the sake of argument — that I happened to be in love with her!

PLATONOV. Then you'd be grateful to me for the chance to run after her and wipe away her tears.

DR TRILETZKY. I sometimes wonder if you're responsible for your actions!

Exit DR TRILETZKY *after* GREKOVA.

SASHA (*reproachfully*): Misha! Please!

GLAGOLYEV. There was a time when we treated women with respect!

COLONEL TRILETZKY. We get her back in, and — bang! — there's her head on the floor all over again!

PLATONOV. Yes. Stupid of me. Stupidity begets stupidity.

SOFYA. And you never could bear stupidity.

PLATONOV (*turns to her*). I'm sorry . . .

SOFYA. I didn't think you were even going to notice me.

PLATONOV. I don't believe we've met.

SOFYA. You don't recognise me, then?

VOYNITZEV (*to* PLATONOV): Careful! This is a serious examination!

COLONEL TRILETZKY. Future career depends upon it!

VOYNITZEV. No? Well, then, may I introduce my wife? Sofya Yegorovna.

PLATONOV. Sofya Yegorovna . . . Your wife?

SOFYA. Have I changed so much?

PLATONOV. No, but . . . here! And you're married? (*To* VOYNITZEV:) This is the lady? Why didn't you say?

VOYNITZEV. A little surprise.

SOFYA. Have you forgotten, Platonov?

VOYNITZEV. A little reminder of your student days.

SOFYA.   I was hardly out of school.

VOYNITZEV. And this is his wife. Alexandra Ivanovna.

SOFYA (*to* SASHA): I'm very pleased to meet you.

VOYNITZEV. The colonel's daughter. And the sister of the wittiest man in the world. Apart from Platonov himself.

SOFYA (*to* PLATONOV): So we're both married?

PLATONOV. I wonder you recognised me. The last five years have ravaged me like rats at a cheese. My life has not turned out as you might have supposed.

VOYNITZEV. She thought you were the second Byron!

COLONEL TRILETZKY. We all thought he was another Newton!

SOFYA. And in fact you're the local schoolmaster?

PLATONOV. Yes.

SOFYA. The local schoolmaster. I find that difficult to believe. Why haven't you . . . done better?

PLATONOV. Why haven't I done better?

VOYNITZEV (*to* PLATONOV): Now *you're* being called to account!

COLONEL TRILETZKY. This makes a change!

PLATONOV. Why haven't I done better? What can I say?

SOFYA. You finished university, at any rate?

VOYNITZEV. No, he gave it up.

COLONEL TRILETZKY. He knew it all. Nothing more they could teach him.

PLATONOV. I got married.

SOFYA. I see. Still, that doesn't stop you leading a decent life, does it?

PLATONOV. A decent life?

COLONEL TRILETZKY. The boot's on the other foot now, and no mistake!

SOFYA. Perhaps I shouldn't have put it like that. But giving up university doesn't stop you doing something worthwhile, does it? It doesn't stop you fighting for political freedom or the emancipation of women? It doesn't stop you serving a cause?

PLATONOV. Oh, dear. What can I say to that?

GLAGOLYEV. I think our Savonarola has met his match!

COLONEL TRILETZKY. Come on, Misha! Return her fire!

PLATONOV. No, she's right. There's nothing to stop me. The question is whether there was ever anything there to be stopped. I wasn't put into this world to do things; I was put here to prevent others from doing them.

    PETRIN *appears in the garden.*

To lie here like some great flat stone and trip them up. To make them stub their toes against me.

SOFYA. And shall you lie in the same place for the rest of your life?

PLATONOV (*indicates* PETRIN). Who's going to hinder people like him, for instance, if I don't do it? Look at him! Anna Petrovna hasn't been back for a day, and already he's round here dunning her.

VOYNITZEV. Platonov — please! Don't start, I beg of you. We went through all this last summer.

PETRIN *comes into the room.*

Gerasim Kuzmich!

They shake hands.

PLATONOV. You were deep in thought out there. What were you contemplating? Life and death? Or bills and promissory notes?

VOYNITZEV (*to* PETRIN): And this is my wife. Sofya Yegorovna.

PETRIN (*to* PLATONOV): Don't talk to me about bills. (*He shakes hands with* SOFYA.) How do you do? (*To* PLATONOV:) Don't talk to me about promissory notes! (*To* VOYNITZEV:) Yes, of course. Congratulations! (*To* PLATONOV:) They're nothing but dreams and delusions, my friend! They say: 'You possess money!' But when you reach out your hand for the money you possess, you find you possess nothing.

PLATONOV (*to* SOFYA): The old general didn't know what he was doing at the end of his life.

PETRIN. Yes, and who was there to help him?

PLATONOV. He didn't know what he was signing.

PETRIN. Who closed his eyes?

PLATONOV (*to* SOFYA). You wonder at me. And rightly so. But there's a whole world for you to wonder at here! A whole new world of fools and knaves.

VOYNITZEV. Now, Platonov . . .

PLATONOV. Sixty taverns, this fine gentleman owns.

PETRIN. Sixty-three.

PLATONOV. I beg your pardon.

PETRIN. And I should think you've drunk in all of them, haven't you?

PLATONOV. A public benefactor. Someone we all touch our caps to.

PETRIN. I am also a member of a learned profession. I am a qualified lawyer! Did you know that? On top of which I'm in the seventh grade of the civil service. And I have lived a little longer than you!

VOYNITZEV. Please!

GLAGOLYEV. No, but it's true! Some of us have lived a little longer than others!

PLATONOV. Wonderful. And what does that prove?

PETRIN. When you get to my age you'll find out!

GLAGOLYEV (*to* PLATONOV): You never knew the past, you see.

PETRIN. To survive your life — that takes some doing!

GLAGOLYEV (*agreeing*): We knew how to enjoy our life!

PETRIN. But there's a price to be paid!

GLAGOLYEV (*agreeing*): We didn't count the cost!

PETRIN (*to* GLAGOLYEV): But what does he know about life?

PLATONOV (*to* PETRIN): What do *you* know about life?

VOYNITZEV. Platonov, please!

PETRIN. No — he wants to know about life — I'll tell him about life.

GLAGOLYEV. It's a question of respect.

PETRIN (*to* PLATONOV): I'll tell you about life. When a man is born he can take any one of three roads, and only three roads — there are no others to be taken.

GLAGOLYEV (*agreeing*): Respect or lack of respect. That's all.

PETRIN. If he goes to the right he'll be eaten by wolves. If he goes to the left he'll eat wolves to survive. And if he goes straight on — he'll end up by eating himself.

GLAGOLYEV. Because we knew how to be happy.

PLATONOV (*to* SOFYA): Look at him, though! They all bend the knee before this jumped-up nobody. And why? Because they're all up to their ears in debt to him!

VOYNITZEV. Now that's enough, Platonov! It's very awkward for the hosts when guests fall out.

PLATONOV (*to* SOFYA): Are you embarrassed by our rural entertainments?

SOFYA. I find it all very illuminating.

VOYNITZEV (*to* PLATONOV): Sometimes you go too far, though.

PETRIN. What have I ever done to him?

PLATONOV. But that's the worst thing of all — that even those with some pretension to honour will say nothing! They all maintain this silence, this deathly silence!

> COLONEL TRILETZKY *snores in his sleep.*

SASHA (*shakes him*): Wake up, Papa! You can't go to sleep here!

COLONEL TRILETZKY. Lunch?

PLATONOV. No. Go back to sleep again.

SASHA. Misha!

> OSIP *appears in the garden, waiting awkwardly.*

PLATONOV. I prefer the company of good honest criminals. (*He calls:*) Osip!

VOYNITZEV. Oh, no!

GLAGOLYEV. Not him again!

PETRIN. What's he going to do — invite him in?

PLATONOV. Come in, Osip.

> OSIP *comes into the room, very out of place. He is concealing something under his shirt.*

PLATONOV (*to* SOFYA): May I introduce my friend Osip?

VOYNITZEV (*resignedly*). Wipe your boots, then Osip.

PLATONOV. Osip is our local horsethief.

VOYNITZEV. What are you doing here, Osip?

OSIP. Nothing, sir. Waiting for the mistress. Say welcome home, like.

VOYNITZEV. Very thoughtful of you, Osip. (*To* SOFYA:) All part of your introduction to local society, I suppose.

COLONEL TRILETZKY. Lives rough, this one.

GLAGOLYEV. In the forest.

PETRIN. Like a wild animal.

PLATONOV. Our local burglar. And murderer. Aren't you, Osip.

OSIP (*to* VOYNITZEV): Came to say congratulations, hope you'll be very happy, sir.

VOYNITZEV. Thank you, Osip.

PLATONOV. Look at that grin! There's a ton of iron in that face!

VOYNITZEV. So what have you been stealing off us this winter, Osip?

OSIP. Haven't been stealing nothing, sir.

VOYNITZEV. No?

OSIP. No, sir. Been away, sir.

VOYNITZEV. Where have you been, Osip?

OSIP. Been in prison, sir.

PLATONOV. Why have you been in prison?

OSIP. Because it's cold in the forest in winter.

PETRIN. Prison! Why have they never packed you off to Siberia for good and all? Look, he's got something hidden under his shirt even now!

VOYNITZEV. What is it, Osip?

OSIP. Nothing, sir.

PLATONOV. Nothing, he says! And nothing is what we do about it! That's why he doesn't go to Siberia! We all know he's a thief — but we all know he's a murderer, too, so no one's got the courage to look inside his shirt. And that's all that stops the rest of them here from going to Siberia! They're all standing here with a bulging wad of nothing stuffed away in their shirts, and no one's got the courage to challenge them!

VOYNITZEV. Platonov, really!

GLAGOLYEV. He's gone too far this time! There is a limit to everything, and he has gone beyond it!

PLATONOV. Sixty-three taverns, this man owns! (*To* OSIP:) I don't suppose you've got sixty-three kopecks. You're only a beginner at thieving!

PETRIN. Are you seriously comparing me with a common horse-thief?

PLATONOV. Certainly not! I wouldn't insult horsethieves!

Uproar, through which COLONEL TRILETZKY *sleeps.*

VOYNITZEV. Please! Please!

PETRIN (*pointing at* PLATONOV). Either he goes or I go!

VOYNITZEV (*to* OSIP): *You* go! You're the cause of all this!

PLATONOV (*pointing at* OSIP): If he goes, I go!

SASHA (*to* PLATONOV): For the love of God! You're shaming me in front of everyone!

Enter ANNA PETROVNA.

ANNA PETROVNA. Stop it! Stop it! It's getting like last year all over again! I won't have it! Platonov, we were all perfectly happy until you arrived!

PLATONOV (*offended*): Oh, you're on their side, are you? You don't want me here, either? In that case I'll go!

PLATONOV *goes out into the garden.*

SASHA (*to* ANNA PETROVNA): I'm so sorry!

ANNA PETROVNA (*to* SASHA): Don't be silly. He'll calm down in a moment. Osip, what are you doing here?

OSIP. Nothing. Say welcome home, like. Brought you a little baby owl. (*He produces it from inside his shirt.*)

ANNA PETROVNA. Oh, how sweet. Take it round to the stables and find a box for it. Then go to the kitchen door and they'll give you something to eat.

   OSIP *goes out into the garden.*

In fact we can all eat. Lunch is served!

SASHA (*to* ANNA PETROVNA): Please forgive him!

ANNA PETROVNA. There's nothing to forgive! It's all over. It's all forgotten.

GLAGOLYEV. We all know what Platonov's like.

VOYNITZEV (*to* SOFYA): Yes, there's your Platonov for you, my love!

SOFYA. I'm afraid I upset him. I shouldn't have spoken so frankly.

GLAGOLYEV. No, no, the man's a crank. (*To* SASHA:) Saving your presence. (*To* SOFYA:) There's no telling what will make him fly up next.

PETRIN. It's like having a performing bear in the house. Will he perform, or will he maul you?

ANNA PETROVNA. Gerasim Kuzmich. I haven't said hello to you.

PETRIN. Anna Petrovna! Could I have a word with you?

ANNA PETROVNA. You'll stay to lunch?

PETRIN. Yes, but if I could just have one word first . . .

ANNA PETROVNA. Where's our performing bear hiding himself now? (*To the others*:) Do go on in to lunch!

ANNA PETROVNA *goes towards the garden, followed by* PETRIN.

PETRIN. If you could just give me some hope . . .

ANNA PETROVNA. After lunch! There's always more hope after lunch.

ANNA PETROVNA *goes out into the garden.*

SASHA (*despairingly*): Father! Please!

COLONEL TRILETZKY (*wakes with a start*). Haven't had lunch, have we?

VOYNITZEV. Come on, Colonel . . .

VOYNITZEV *helps* COLONEL TRILETZKY *out.* GLAGOLYEV *begins to usher* SOFYA *and* SASHA *out after him.*

SASHA. I'm sorry. I'm sorry.

GLAGOLYEV. No, no! What should we do without the colonel and his family to entertain us?

Exeunt SOFYA *and* SASHA. GLAGOLYEV *is detained by* PETRIN.

PETRIN. Just tell me. Did you?

GLAGOLYEV. Did I what?

PETRIN. Did you ask her?

GLAGOLYEV. Not yet.

PETRIN. My dear fellow! What are you waiting for? The colonel will get in ahead of you!

GLAGOLYEV. The colonel? The colonel hasn't got two kopecks for a candle!

PETRIN. He's got kopecks enough to buy skyrockets for her! Behind the old summerhouse — Yakov showed me. Might say more to a woman than flowers! You do want to marry her?

GLAGOLYEV. I'm not averse to the idea.

PETRIN. Well, then.

GLAGOLYEV. But will *she* want to marry *me*? That could be the difficulty, you see.

PETRIN. Of course she will!

GLAGOLYEV. Will she? Which of us knows the secrets of another's heart?

PETRIN. Lovely woman — handsome man. You're made for each other! Shall I ask her for you?

GLAGOLYEV. I can do my own courting, thank you! What's it to do with you?

PETRIN. A man needs a wife, Porfiry Semyonovich! An estate needs a man! And debts need someone to pay them! I don't want to take her to court and force her to sell up! I'm a reasonable man, Porfiry Semyonovich! All I want is my money!

    ANNA PETROVNA *appears in the garden, her arm in* PLATONOV'*s.*

Here she is, Porfiry Semyonovich! Ask her now!

GLAGOLYEV (*hesitates*). I can't do it on an empty stomach. Lunch first!

PETRIN. Your happiness — that's all I want! Your happiness and my money.

    Exeunt GLAGOLYEV *and* PETRIN *in the direction of lunch.*

    Enter ANNA PETROVNA *and* PLATONOV *from the garden.*

ANNA PETROVNA. But I *can't* get rid of them, you see. Nor can you, for all your eloquence. I depend upon them! It's like a very complicated position on a chess board. If I didn't make Porfiry Semyonovich just a little bit jealous of the colonel . . . if I didn't make the colonel just a little bit jealous of the doctor . . . if I wasn't protected from the doctor by poor little Grekova . . . if Petrin didn't believe he'd get his

money from Glagolyev . . . if you weren't here to lighten my
heart . . . why, then the queen would fall. I should lose the
estate, Platonov! I should lose everything. Then what would
you do? Any of you? The lion must roar — of course he
must — but a little more softly, Platonov, or he'll roar the
whole house down. Yes? Now you wait here. I'm going to send
Marya Yefimovna out to you. I found *her* in tears, Platonov!
So you're going to give her your paw and apologise.

> *Enter* VOYNITZEV.

VOYNITZEV. Come on! They're all waiting to drink our health!

ANNA PETROVNA. He's got something else to do first. (*To*
PLATONOV:) Now, wait! Don't you dare come into lunch
until you've done as I told you!

> *Exit* ANNA PETROVNA.

VOYNITZEV. What's all this?

PLATONOV. I'm offering my paw to get my lunch . . . Sergey,
you're a lucky man. She's a lovely woman, your Sofya. Are
you happy?

VOYNITZEV. I don't know . . .

PLATONOV. You don't know?

VOYNITZEV. Are you and Sasha happy?

PLATONOV. We're a family! We've made a nest! One of these
days you'll understand what that means. Take Sasha away
from me and I think I should be finished. Utterly destroyed.
We're the perfect couple — she's a fool and I'm a rogue. *Aren't*
you happy?

VOYNITZEV. I suppose we are. I suppose this is what being
happy is.

> *Enter* DR TRILETZKY, *eating, glass in one hand, bottle in
> the other.*

PLATONOV (*to* DR TRILETZKY). You've been stuffing yourself
already, then. Have you forgiven me?

DR TRILETZKY. What for? Come on! We've got to drink to the great homecoming. (*He puts his arm round* PLATONOV.) Drink, drink, drink!

PLATONOV. Have you seen your patients today?

DR TRILETZKY (*moves away from him*). Misha, once and for all, if you're going to lecture me, let's make a regular arrangement. Private moral coaching, an hour a day, four to five, and I'll pay you a ruble a time!

VOYNITZEV (*puts his arms round both of them*). Come on, my friends, let's go and drink Bruderschaft together! Then fate can do its worst. To hell with moneylenders, to hell with creditors! Just so long as all the people I love in this world are alive and well. You're all I have!

DR TRILETZKY. We're all we all have!

Enter GREKOVA. *She stops at the sight of them.*

PLATONOV. Come on! I'm going to drink to everything, with everything there is to drink! I haven't been drunk for a long, long time, and I'm going to get drunk today!

They start to go, but stop at the sight of GREKOVA.

PLATONOV. Marya Yefimovna! I apologise. I publicly beg your forgiveness. I burn with shame. Give me your hand . . . I go down on one knee and publicly kiss your hand!

GREKOVA snatches her hand back.

And now she's going to start snivelling again!

Exit GREKOVA *in tears.*

Come back here, Beetle-juice!

Exit PLATONOV *after her.*

DR TRILETZKY. Misha, I implore you!

VOYNITZEV. Can you *never* be serious?

Exeunt DR TRILETZKY *and* VOYNITZEV *after him. A piano, off, strikes up a cheerful dance. The row of windows is shifted aside to begin:-*

Scene Two

The garden. As in the previous scene, less the windows. The light mellows. Enter YAKOV *and* VASILY, *who change the drawing-room chairs for garden chairs, as if dancing with them in time to the music. Enter* SASHA, *carrying something concealed beneath a napkin. She turns guiltily aside to hide it from* YAKOV, *and comes face to face with* VASILY. *For a moment she is involved ridiculously in the dance. Then the music ends, and* YAKOV *and* VASILY *usher the last two chairs off.*

SASHA (*calls, softly*). Where are you? Are you there?

> OSIP *emerges from the trees.* SASHA *takes the napkin off what she is holding; it is a plate of food.*

OSIP. We're both thieves, then. (*He takes the plate, sits down, and eats hungrily with his fingers.*)

SASHA. Take your cap off. It's a sin to eat with your head covered. And you say a little grace, now!

> OSIP *removes his cap, and continues to eat. There is the distant whistle of a train.*

There — that's the evening train. It'll be dark soon. And they still haven't finished lunch! Eating, drinking. Singing, dancing. Then eating and drinking again. My head's ringing . . . And they couldn't find a few scraps in the kitchen for you . . .? Well, God be with them . . . As soon as it's dark we'll be having the fireworks. I haven't seen fireworks since I was a girl. Not since people gave parties for all the officers, when my father had his regiment . . .

> *Another train whistle, a little nearer, and then for a moment the faint sound of the locomotive.*

There it goes. Over the crossing. Past our little house . . .

> *Pause.* OSIP *hands the plate back to* SASHA *and wipes his mouth.*

OSIP. I kissed her once.

SASHA. Anna Petrovna? You kissed her? (*She sits beside him.*)

OSIP. Hot summer's day. Like today. In the forest here. I'm going along this track and I look round and there she is, she's standing in a little stream and she's holding her dress up with one hand and she's scooping up water in a dock leaf with the other. She scoops. She drinks. Scoops. Drinks. Scoops again, and pours it over her head. It's one of those days when you can feel the air heavy on you, and you can't hear nothing but the buzzing of the flies ... She pays no heed to me. Just another peasant, she thinks. So I go down to the edge of the stream, right close up to her, as close as I am to you now, and I just look at her. Like this, like I'm looking at you. And she stands there in the water in front of me, with her skirts up in her hand, and she bends, she scoops, she pours. And the water runs over her hair, over her face and her neck, then down over her dress, and all she says is: 'What are you staring at, idiot? Haven't you ever seen a human being before?' And she scoops and she pours, and I just stand gazing. Then suddenly she turns and gives me a sharp look. 'Oh,' she says, 'you've taken a fancy to me, have you?' And I say: 'I reckon I could kiss you and die.' So that made her laugh. 'All right,' she says, 'you can kiss me if you like.' Well, I felt as if I'd been thrown into a furnace. I went up to her — into the stream, boots and all, I didn't think twice — and I took her by the shoulder, very lightly, and I kissed her right here, on her cheek, and here on her neck, as hard as ever I could.

SASHA. So what did she do then?

OSIP. 'Now, then,' she says, 'be off with you! And you wash a little more often,' she says, 'and you do something about your nails!' And off I went.

SASHA. She's a bold one, all right.

OSIP. After that you'd have thought I'd gone mad. Couldn't eat. Couldn't sleep. Everywhere I went I could see her in front of me. Shut my eyes — there she was again. I must have looked right soft. I wanted to go round and shoot the poor old general! And then when she was widowed I started doing all kinds of little things for her. Shot partridges for her — caught quails — painted that old summerhouse of hers all different colours. Took her a live wolf once. She'd only to say and I'd have done it. Told me to eat myself and I'd have eaten myself . . . Took her a baby hare last year. She holds it in her arms, and she strokes it, and she says to me, 'Is it true what they say about you, Osip — that you're a bandit?' 'As true as I'm standing here,' I tell her. 'Then we're going to have to reform you,' she says. 'You'll have to go off on a pilgrimage. All the way to Kiev on foot. Then on to Moscow, and a year from now you'll be a different man.' Well, I got myself up like a beggar, I slung my bag on my back, and off I went to Kiev. Wasn't no use, though. Hadn't got no further than Kharkov when I fell in with a whole company of pilgrims. And what did I do? I drank my money, got into a fight, lost my papers, and came home again, Now she won't let me do nothing for her.

> ANNA PETROVNA *appears among the trees in the background. She moves irresolutely first in this direction and then in that, looking for someone.*

SASHA. There she is . . . She'll see you.

OSIP. Why should I care?

SASHA. It's true, though. When you're soft on someone there's nothing to be done with you. When I first loved Platonov and still didn't know that he loved me I went through terrible torments. Wandered about the forest like a lost soul.

OSIP. And now what does he do? He dangles round her ladyship! Not much heart, that husband of yours. Got the brains, though, and he's got the words. He could have the whole female race after him if he wanted.

SASHA. That's enough now. I don't like that kind of talk.

VOYNITZEV (*calls, off*). Sofya! Sofya!

DR TRILETZKY (*calls, off*). Misha! Where are you?

ANNA PETROVNA *vanishes.*

SASHA. Now they're all coming out. They'll find you, for sure. Anyway, it's no good sitting here moping after her. That won't get you anywhere.

OSIP. Why should he want more women after him, though? He's got the best of them already.

OSIP *melts away beneath the trees as* VOYNITZEV *enters.*

SASHA. Is it time for the fireworks?

VOYNITZEV. Yes, but I've lost Sofya.

SASHA. I'll fetch Platonov. You won't start without us, will you?

VOYNITZEV. I thought she was in the garden.

Enter DR TRILETZKY, *noticeably drunk.*

Have you seen Sofya?

DR TRILETZKY. No. Looking for Misha.

VOYNITZEV (*calls*): Sofya . . . !

Exit VOYNITZEV.

DR TRILETZKY (*calls*): Misha! (*To* SASHA:) I've got a ruble for him! Have a ruble, Sasha . . . (*He sees the empty plate in her hand.*) Poor Sasha! Eating out here on your own! Have two rubles, Sasha! Have three!

SASHA (*brushes the money aside*). Oh, no! Are you as drunk as that?

DR TRILETZKY. I'm not drunk, Sasha! It's Gerasim Kuzmich who's drunk! Gave me all his money to look after! 'If I don't give this to you,' he said, 'I know I'll only go and give it to someone else.' (*He sniffs the money.*) Peasant money . . . Here — four rubles for my lovely sister. And if you think I'm drunk you want to see Father!

SASHA. What have I done to deserve this? Where is he?

DR TRILETZKY. Behind the sofa.

SASHA. No use expecting any help from you, I suppose. Where's Misha?

DR TRILETZKY. I can't find him!

SASHA. Well, find him! I'll find Father.

> *Exit* SASHA.

DR TRILETZKY (*calls*). Misha! Misha!

> *Exit* DR TRILETZKY.
> *Enter* SOFYA *from under the trees. She sits down on one of the garden seats.*

VOYNITZEV (*calls, off*). Sofya! Where are you?

DR TRILETZKY (*calls, off*). A reward of one ruble for anyone who finds Platonov!

> *Enter* PLATONOV *from the same direction as* SOFYA.

PLATONOV. I follow you into the living-room — you go back into the dining-room. I go into the dining-room — you go into the garden. I come into the garden — you run back towards the house.

SOFYA. You keep talking about the past. What does it matter? A student loved a schoolgirl; a schoolgirl loved a student. It's an old story! Old and trite! Too old and trite for it to mean much to us now.

PLATONOV. Then what are you so frightened of?

SOFYA. I'm not frightened of anything!

PLATONOV. Is every man you meet really such a threat to your Sergey? If I've talked to you too much this evening, if I've wearied you with my attentions, then it's because you're an intelligent and sympathetic woman. What do you think? That I want to take you away from your husband? That I'm in love with you? That you've somehow made a conquest of the local intellectual? Tamed the village eccentric? How wonderful! What bliss! What a nice box of chocolates for our little egotist!

SOFYA. You've gone mad.

PLATONOV. Run away, then! Run back to him! No one's forcing you to stay here!

Pause.

So hot, even now . . . I shouldn't have drunk so much . . .

Pause.

Why haven't I done better? The first thing you asked me! Not 'Are you well?' or 'Are you happy?' Not at all! 'Why haven't you done better?'

SOFYA. I'm sorry.

PLATONOV. No, you're right. Why haven't I? Teeming evil all around me, fouling the earth, swallowing up my brothers in Christ, while I sit here with folded hands. I shall be the same when I'm forty, the same when I'm fifty. I shan't change now. Not until I decline into shuffling old age, and stupefied indifference to everything outside my own body. A wasted life! Then death. And when I think of that death I'm terrified.

Pause.

Why haven't I done better? I might ask the same of you. What's happened to that pure heart you used to have? Where's the old sincerity, the truthfulness, the boldness? You ask me why I haven't done better; do you ever ask your husband? You've let the years go by in idleness. You watch others callous their hands and hearts on your behalf. And still you manage to meet their eye. That is depravity.

SOFYA *gets to her feet.*
PLATONOV *makes her sit down again.*

One last word, and then I'll let you go. You were so splendid once! No, let me finish . . . You were good. You had greatness in you. (*He takes her hand.*) What in all the wide world made you marry that man?

SOFYA. Sergey? He's a fine man!

PLATONOV. He's a moral pygmy!

SOFYA. He's my husband!

PLATONOV. He's bogged down in debt — he's helpless with doing nothing!

SOFYA. Lower your voice, will you! There are people about!

PLATONOV. I don't care! Let them all hear! (*Quietly*:) I'm sorry if I spoke sharply. I loved you, though. Loved you more than all the world. This hair. These hands. This face . . . And what can you do here? You'll only go deeper and deeper into the mire. Why do we never lead the life we have it in us to lead? If I had the strength I should uproot us from this mudhole — uproot us both! We'd leave! Tonight! Take the night train and never return!

SOFYA. What are you saying?

PLATONOV. You know what I'm saying. . .

    Enter PETRIN *and* GLAGOLYEV, *both a little bit drunk.*

PETRIN (*to* GLAGOLYEV): Put a ruble in front of me and I'll steal it!

    SOFYA *flees into the depths of the garden.*

PLATONOV. Sofya! (*He runs after her.*)

PETRIN. I should, Porfiry! I'd steal it! I honestly should! If I thought I could get away with it! Put a ruble in front of *you* and you'd steal it!

GLAGOLYEV. I shouldn't, Gerasya! I shouldn't, you know!

PETRIN. Twenty thousand rubles, then.

GLAGOLYEV. No, no!

PETRIN. Fifty thousand!

GLAGOLYEV. No, no, no.

PETRIN. Show me an honest man, Porfiry, and I'll show you a fool!

GLAGOLYEV. I'm a fool, Gerasya!

PETRIN (*sadly*): Yes. You're a fool. And it's no good just sitting in there and staring at her! What kind of way is that to win a woman? You were just sitting there like a mushroom!

GLAGOLYEV. I'll win her, Gerasya, never you fear! I'll marry her yet!

PETRIN. Yes, but when, Porfiry, when? Who knows how long we've got, at our age? Ask her tonight. Porfiry! It's a beautiful summer's night. And she's in love! Didn't you see her laughing at lunch? Didn't you see the wild look in her eye? Here she comes. Look at her! Look at her!

> *Enter* ANNA PETROVNA *and* GREKOVA, *in the depths of the garden.*

She's followed you out here.

GLAGOLYEV. She's got Marya Yefimovna with her.

ANNA PETROVNA (*calls*): Doctor! Doctor?

PETRIN. She's trying to get rid of her. She wants to be alone.

DR TRILETZKY (*calls, off*): Misha! Where are you, Misha?

> ANNA PETROVNA *urges* GREKOVA *off in the direction of the voice.*

PETRIN. You see? She's waiting for you! Quick! Before the colonel comes out! One more glass to get his courage up and he'll go into battle! You'll never have another chance like this!

> ANNA PETROVNA, *now that* GREKOVA *is out of sight, goes off purposefully in another direction.*

After her, then, Porfiry! Steal that ruble!

> *Exit* GLAGOLYEV *uncertainly after* ANNA PETROVNA. *Enter* VOYNITZEV.

VOYNITZEV. I've lost Sofya. I can't understand it . . . (*He looks off in the direction taken by* ANNA PETROVNA.) That isn't her, is it?

PETRIN. No, no! That way, that way!

> *He directs* VOYNITZEV *in some other direction, then goes off anxiously after* GLAGOLYEV. *Enter* GREKOVA.

GREKOVA (*to* VOYNITZEV): Platonov?

VOYNITZEV. Sofya?

GREKOVA. I'm sorry.

VOYNITZEV. I beg your pardon.

> *Exit* GREKOVA, *in some confusion.*
> *Enter* SOFYA, *in some agitation.*

SOFYA. Sergey!

VOYNITZEV. Sofya! I thought I'd lost you forever! Where have you been?

SOFYA. Let's go away from here!

VOYNITZEV. Away?

SOFYA. Anywhere! Abroad!

VOYNITZEV. If you like.

SOFYA. Now!

VOYNITZEV. Now?

SOFYA. Tonight.

VOYNITZEV. Sofya!

SOFYA. Please, Sergey!

VOYNITZEV. But . . . but . . . what about the fireworks?

SOFYA. No — no fireworks!

VOYNITZEV. Sofya, my love, I know how dull it is for you here . . .

SOFYA. There's a train. There's a night train.

VOYNITZEV. My love, we're not *that* boring! Not all of us, anyway. I'm sure it would help if you talked to Platonov.

SOFYA. Platonov?

> *Enter* PLATONOV *at the sound of his name. He stops at the sight of* VOYNITZEV, *and stands at the edge of the trees, unnoticed, watching them.*

VOYNITZEV. I know you're disappointed in him. I saw you avoiding him all afternoon. And he has become a bit of a bear, I admit. But he's not like the others. He's someone I love. He's someone you'll love, too, when you know him a little better. Come on, let's find him!

SOFYA. Sergey, please listen . . .

VOYNITZEV. No, no — you listen to Platonov. I know he'll persuade you to stay! At least until we've had the fireworks!

> *Exeunt* VOYNITZEV *and* SOFYA.
> PLATONOV *goes to follow them.*
> *Enter* ANNA PETROVNA.

ANNA PETROVNA. And here he is. Our philosopher. Shunning us all. Pacing the garden and thinking his own thoughts. But what a perfect summer's night! Cool air at last. And the first star . . . What a pity ladies aren't supposed to sleep outside under the open sky. When I was a little girl I always slept in the garden in summer.

> *Pause.*

You've got a new tie.

PLATONOV. Yes.

ANNA PETROVNA. I'm in such an odd mood today . . . I feel pleased with everything . . . Say something, Platonov!

PLATONOV. What do you want me to say?

ANNA PETROVNA. I want to hear the sound of your voice. I want to hear it saying — I don't know — something new, something sharp, something sweet. Because you're being terribly clever today, and you're looking terribly handsome, and I'm more in love with you than ever. And you're being so nice! You're causing scarcely any trouble at all!

PLATONOV. I've never seen you looking more lovely.

ANNA PETROVNA. Are we friends, Platonov?

PLATONOV. Of course. If we're not friends, who is?

ANNA PETROVNA. Real friends? Great friends?

PLATONOV. What is this? We're friends, we're friends! You're behaving like a schoolgirl!

ANNA PETROVNA. So, we're friends. But you know, do you, my dear sir, that from friendship between a man and a woman it's only a short step to love?

PLATONOV. Is it indeed? You and I shall not be taking that one step to perdition, however short it may be.

ANNA PETROVNA. So you see love as perdition, do you? I see it as something noble. Why should we be ashamed of it? Why shouldn't we take that one short step?

PLATONOV (*stares at her*). Let's go inside and dance, shall we?

ANNA PETROVNA. You can't dance! I think it's time you and I had a little talk. I don't know quite where to begin, though. You're such a difficult man! Now try to listen for once, and not to philosophise ... (*She sits.*) Sit down ... Look, he's quite embarrassed! It's all right, my dear — your wife can't hear us!

PLATONOV. Perhaps I should say something first.

ANNA PETROVNA. Perhaps you should.

PLATONOV. It's not worth it. I promise you, Anna Petrovna — it's simply not worth it.

ANNA PETROVNA. Isn't it? Now you listen to me. Sit down ... Sit down!

He sits beside her.

Look, if you were free, I shouldn't think twice — I'd make myself your wife. I'd bestow my rank and station on you. But as it is ...

Pause.

Am I to take your silence as a sign of agreement?

Pause.

I think in the circumstances it is a little ungentlemanly of you not to say *something*.

PLATONOV (*jumps to his feet*). Let's forget this conversation! Let's pretend it never took place!

ANNA PETROVNA. You are a clown, Misha.

PLATONOV. I respect you! And I respect in myself the respect I have for you! I'm not against harmless diversion . . .

ANNA PETROVNA. I know, Platonov.

PLATONOV. But not with a beautiful, intelligent, untrammelled woman like you! What — a month or two of foolishness, and then to go our ways in shame? I couldn't do it!

ANNA PETROVNA. I wasn't talking about foolishness. I was talking about love.

PLATONOV. And do you think I don't love you? I love you for your goodness, for your generous heart. I love you desperately — I love you to distraction! I'll lay down my life for you, if that's what you want! Does every love have to be reduced to the same common denominator? I love you as a woman, yes, but I also love you as a person. On top of which, my dear, I am just a tiny bit married.

ANNA PETROVNA (*rises*). You've also had just a tiny bit too much to drink, and you're being just a tiny bit hypocritical. Go on, then. When your head's clear we'll have another talk.

PLATONOV. No, the trouble is, I can't hide my true feelings from you. (*Quietly and intimately.*) If I could, my precious, I should long since have been your lover.

Exit PLATONOV.

ANNA PETROVNA (*to herself*): Intolerable man! (*She calls.*) Come back here! Misha! Misha . . .

She is about to run after him when GLAGOLYEV *enters suddenly from among the trees.*

GLAGOLYEV. Anna Petrovna!

ANNA PETROVNA. Oh! You quite startled me!

GLAGOLYEV. Anna Petrovna, you know, I believe, in what high regard I hold your sex. I have more than once been accused of romanticism, but for me a world without women would be akin to a paradise without angels. And yet such is the world,

during the winter months at any rate, in which I myself live.
Anna Petrovna . . .

COLONEL TRILETZKY (*calls, off*). Anna Petrovna!

ANNA PETROVNA. I'm afraid we've been spotted by the artillery.

GLAGOLYEV. Yes. I'll come straight to the point, then. Anna
Petrovna, will you be the angel in my paradise?

COLONEL TRILETZKY (*off*). You're getting my feet all muddled
up! Perfectly all right on my own!

ANNA PETROVNA (*watching* COLONEL TRILETZKY's
approach). Any angel who took wing in these parts would
almost certainly end up filled with shot by the colonel.

> GLAGOLYEV *turns to watch* COLONEL TRILETZKY.
> *Exit* ANNA PETROVNA *in the opposite direction.*

GLAGOLYEV. The colonel himself appears to be filled with
something rather stronger than shot . . . (*He becomes aware
that* ANNA PETROVNA *has departed.*) Anna Petrovna!

> *Enter* PETRIN *from behind the trees.*

PETRIN. That way!

> *Exit* GLAGOLYEV *after* ANNA PETROVNA, *and* PETRIN
> *after* GLAGOLYEV.

> *Enter* COLONEL TRILETZKY, *drunk, attended by* DR
> TRILETZKY *and* SASHA. DR TRILETZKY, *who is
> wearing the officer's peaked cap in which his father arrived,
> is amused by the colonel's condition.*

COLONEL TRILETZKY. Don't push me! Don't push me! (*He
discovers he is not being pushed.*) Oh, you're there.

SASHA. If you've no fear before God you might at least have
some shame in front of other people! Everyone staring at you!
Everyone laughing at you! (*To* DR TRILETZKY:) It's nothing
to laugh about!

DR TRILETZKY. Where's Misha, though?

COLONEL TRILETZKY. Where's Anna Petrovna?

SASHA. Vanished at the sight of you, of course.

COLONEL TRILETZKY. Something I wanted to ask her.

DR TRILETZKY. He's forgotten what it was!

SASHA. It's not funny, Kolya!

COLONEL TRILETZKY. What was I saying?

DR TRILETZKY. You could have been a general.

SASHA. Don't encourage him!

COLONEL TRILETZKY. Yes! Another five years or so, and I could have been a general! If I'd been five years older when I reached retiring age . . . No, if I'd been five years younger when I was born . . . What do I mean?

SASHA. Come on — home. You shouldn't be allowed inside a decent house. You're an old man! You should be setting the others an example!

COLONEL TRILETZKY. You're just like your mother! Do you know that? Day and night she used to go on. This isn't right, that isn't right . . . Just like your poor old dear departed mother, my pet! Same yes, same hair. Same way of waddling like a goose . . . (*He kisses her.*) God, how I loved her!

SASHA. That's enough, now. Come on!

COLONEL TRILETZKY. I will, my love. Whatever you say. I haven't always been a good man, Sasha. But I loved your mother. And I never took money from anyone.

DR TRILETZKY. Have another ruble. (*He gives him one.*)

COLONEL TRILETZKY. I'll take it from you because you're my own son. But I've never robbed my country, I've never robbed my friends. All I had to do was to dip my hand in with the rest of them and I could have been rich and famous . . . I could have been a general!

SASHA. Kolya, give him his hat back before he catches cold.

DR TRILETZKY. Where are you off to, then, general?

COLONEL TRILETZKY. I'm seeing this little lady home.

SASHA (*to* DR TRILETZKY): Tell Misha I've gone, when you find him.

DR TRILETZKY. What about the fireworks?

SASHA. I'll just have to wait for another time.

COLONEL TRILETZKY. I'll see her home, then I'll slip back for the fireworks . . . Something I wanted to ask Anna Petrovna . . . Where's Sasha? Oh, you're there. Right, then, quick march . . .! Not so fast, not so fast . . . I'll tell you what. I'll carry you.

SASHA. Don't be silly.

COLONEL TRILETZKY. I'll carry you! Always used to carry your mother. Couldn't walk straight myself — still pick her up and carry her! Come on!

SASHA. Certainly not. Put your cap on properly. (*She straightens his cap for him.*) Smarten you up a bit.

COLONEL TRILETZKY. We rolled all the way down a hill together once. Never said a word about it, poor love. Just laughed, bless her.

> *Exit* COLONEL TRILETZKY, *supported by* SASHA. *Enter* VOYNITZEV.

VOYNITZEV. Where's Platonov? I can't find him anywhere.

DR TRILETZKY. Nor can I. Have another ruble instead. Is it the fireworks?

VOYNITZEV. There won't be any fireworks if I can't find Platonov.

DR TRILETZKY. Won't be any . . . ? (*He calls.*) Misha!

VOYNITZEV (*calls*): Misha!

> *A cry from* COLONEL TRILETZKY, *off.*

SASHA (*off*): *Now* what?

COLONEL TRILETZKY (*off*): I've gone blind!

SASHA (*off*): You've got your cap over your eyes.

VOYNITZEV (*calls*): Misha!

DR TRILETZKY (*calls*): Misha!

> *Exeunt* VOYNITZEV *and* DR TRILETZKY.
> *Enter* PLATONOV *and* SOFYA.

PLATONOV. Going?

SOFYA. Tonight.

PLATONOV. Forever?

SOFYA. Forever.

PLATONOV. What did you tell Sergey?

SOFYA. Nothing.

PLATONOV. What did he say?

SOFYA. He told me to talk to you.

PLATONOV. To *me?*

SOFYA. He said you'd persuade me to stay.

> *Pause. They look at each other.*

PLATONOV. Go.

SOFYA. Go?

PLATONOV. Tonight. At once. You're right — it's the only way. Otherwise I can't answer for the consequences.

> *Pause. They stand looking at each other.*
> *Enter* GREKOVA.

GREKOVA. Platonov . . .

> *She stops at the sight of* SOFYA. *But* SOFYA *suddenly turns and flees.*

I'm sorry. But I can't bear this any longer. You seem to be following me! Everywhere I go — there you are! *Are* you following me?

PLATONOV. Beetle-juice! Come here, you lovely creature!

GREKOVA. What? (*She crosses to him nervously.*)

PLATONOV. You weird and wonderful woman! (*He kisses her.*)

GREKOVA. Why are you kissing me?

PLATONOV. I've got to kiss someone!

GREKOVA. Do you . . . do you love me, then?

PLATONOV. Why, do you love me, you foolish headstrong woman?

GREKOVA. I don't know. That depends on whether you . . .

> *He kisses her.*

You shouldn't do that if you don't.

> *He kisses her.*

Do you love me?

PLATONOV. Not at all, my precious! That's why I'm kissing you!

> *She bursts into tears, flees, and runs into* DR TRILETZKY.

DR TRILETZKY. And here he is! The man everyone wants to see!

GREKOVA. *I* never want to see him again! And if you have any respect for me at all — if you have any respect for yourself — you'll never see him again, either.

DR TRILETZKY. But he's my brother-in-law!

GREKOVA. Yes, everything's a joke to you, too, isn't it. Well, you joke away together, then. That's all you can ever do!

DR TRILETZKY. Have a ruble.

> GREKOVA *turns to flee, with a cry of pain, but is stopped by* VOYNITZEV *as he enters.*

VOYNITZEV. Fireworks!

GREKOVA. What?

VOYNITZEV. Don't run away! (*To* PLATONOV:) We're staying! I don't know what you said, but you persuaded her! I *told* her you were the most eloquent man in the world! I won't forget this, Misha. Come on! I'm going to light the fireworks!

GREKOVA (*to* DR TRILETZKY): I'm going to watch the fireworks, I don't care about you.

> *Exit* VOYNITZEV, *with* GREKOVA *after him.*
> *Enter* ANNA PETROVNA.

DR TRILETZKY (*excited*). Fireworks! Fireworks!

> *Exit* DR TRILETZKY.

PLATONOV (*to* ANNA PETROVNA): My God! What have I done?

ANNA PETROVNA. Sasha's gone. She'll miss the fireworks.

PLATONOV (*takes* ANNA PETROVNA'*s hands in his*). What's going to become of us all?

ANNA PETROVNA. You seem just a tiny bit less married.

PLATONOV. How are we going to survive our lives?

ANNA PETROVNA. First of all by enjoying the fireworks.

> ANNA PETROVNA *begins to lead* PLATONOV *off after the others.*
> *Enter* GLAGOLYEV.

GLAGOLYEV. Anna Petrovna!

> *She turns back to him.*

Let me say at once that I should renounce the usual rights of a husband . . .

ANNA PETROVNA. And let me say one word to you, my friend.

GLAGOLYEV. Yes?

ANNA PETROVNA. Fireworks!

> *Exit* ANNA PETROVNA *after* PLATONOV.
> *Enter* PETRIN.

PETRIN. What did she say? What did she say?

GLAGOLYEV. She said fireworks.

Exit GLAGOLYEV *after* ANNA PETROVNA, *and* PETRIN *after* GLAGOLYEV.
Enter SOFYA.

SOFYA (*to herself*): Is it ruin, or is it happiness? Is it the beginning of a new life, or is it the end of everything?

Enter COLONEL TRILETZKY.

COLONEL TRILETZKY. It's the fireworks!

Exeunt COLONEL TRILETZKY *and* SOFYA *after the others.*
Enter OSIP *from under the trees.*

VOYNITZEV (*off*): Look out, everyone! We're starting!

OSIP *whips out a long-bladed hunting knife; and at the same moment there is the whoosh of a rocket taking off.* OSIP *stands gazing upwards, knife raised, as the coloured stars burst in the sky. There is a collective sigh of satisfaction from the spectators, off. The stars fade.* OSIP *brings the knife down into the back of one of the garden chairs.*

Blackout.

Act Two

Scene One

A clearing in the forest. Right — the local schoolhouse. In the background — the same tall trees as in the previous act. Here, though, they are bisected not by a grassy garden walk, but by a railway line, which comes straight down to the front of the stage, where it passes between the wooden baulks of a rough level crossing.

In the darkness before the scene commences there is the sound of a goods train, clanking and whistling as it passes through the auditorium. The red tail light of the train appears at the front of the stage, moving away from us. The stage lights come up to reveal the smoke left by the locomotive, with the tail light disappearing amongst it. PLATONOV emerges from the smoke, stepping over the rail on to the track, and walking dejectedly towards us. When the smoke finally clears it reveals a brilliant moonlit night, as bright as day.

PLATONOV (*calls, gloomily*). Sasha . . . ! Sasha . . . !

> *A window in the schoolhouse opens, and SASHA looks out, in her nightgown.*

SASHA. Misha?

PLATONOV. Sasha . . .

SASHA. Sh! You'll wake the baby.

PLATONOV. Sasha . . .

SASHA. Are you drunk?

PLATONOV. Sasha, do you love me?

SASHA. Wait. I'll come out.

> *The window closes. PLATONOV sinks gloomily down on to the step of the schoolhouse verandah. The door opens, and SASHA comes out.*

SASHA. What's the time? Was that the goods or the passenger? Are the fireworks over?

PLATONOV. Do you, Sasha?

SASHA. You are a bit drunk. Aren't you, Misha?

PLATONOV. Do you love me?

SASHA. Misha! It took me hours to get him to sleep!

PLATONOV. Do you, though? I want to know.

SASHA. Of course I love you.

PLATONOV. Why?

SASHA. Why?

PLATONOV. Name one single good thing in me that you love me for! Name one good quality that could possibly make me love you!

SASHA. You're in a funny mood, aren't you, Misha? Obviously I love you! You're my husband!

PLATONOV. That's the only reason you love me, because I'm your husband?

SASHA. Misha, sometimes I don't understand you at all.

PLATONOV. Don't you? (*He laughs.*) No, you're a fool, aren't you. A complete fool. You should have been a fly. In the land of the flies, with your brains, you'd have been the cleverest fly of all. (*He kisses her brow.*) Where should we be if you understood me, if you realised how little there was to love in me?

SASHA. What happened? Didn't you enjoy the fireworks?

PLATONOV. Fireworks, fireworks . . . I ran away, Sasha!

SASHA. From the fireworks?

PLATONOV. From myself! Fled, in shame and terror! Came running all the way back to you!

SASHA (*laughs*). You're the fool, Misha!

PLATONOV. And I'm not drunk. I'm not drunk now. I certainly wasn't drunk then.

SASHA. When?

PLATONOV. When I told her she'd married a moral pygmy.

SASHA. Told who? Told Sofya Yegorovna?

PLATONOV. My tongue ran away with me! I behaved like a schoolboy! Postured, strutted, showed off . . .

SASHA. She's beautiful.

PLATONOV. Why did I say all those things? I didn't believe them! *She* believed them, though!

SASHA. I don't think I've ever seen anyone as beautiful as that.

PLATONOV. They found Porfiry Semyonovich in the old summer-house. He'd had a heart attack.

SASHA. Is he all right?

PLATONOV. Your brother bled him. Then he and Gerasim Kuzmich took him home.

SASHA. They want my brother in the village. It's the storekeeper — he's very poorly. Had Kolya sobered up at all?

PLATONOV. I grandly mock people like Porfiry Semyonovich and Gerasim Kuzmich. But who's going to mock me? When are they going to start? It's ridiculous! I don't take bribes, I don't steal, I don't beat my wife, I think high-minded thoughts — and still I'm a scoundrel, a ridiculous scoundrel!

SASHA. Misha, you're talking nonsense. It's time you were in bed.

PLATONOV. Oh, my precious! My lovely silly little noodle! I shouldn't think of you as a wife — I should put you in a glass case with a label on you. How did you and I ever manage to bring a baby into the world? You shouldn't be bearing children, my love; you should still be making little men out of dough. (*He tries to kiss her.*)

SASHA (*refuses to be kissed*). Get away from me! Why did you marry me, if I was such a fool? I didn't force you to! You should have got yourself a clever one, if that's what you wanted! I'm going back to bed.

Exit SASHA *into the house.*

PLATONOV (*laughs*). Oh, and she can manage to lose her temper sometimes! But this is a great discovery! She's learning how to lose her little temper!

He begins to follow her into the house.

All hurt and cross, are we . . . ?

Enter ANNA PETROVNA *from the shadows of the forest. She is wearing a riding habit.*

ANNA PETROVNA. Platonov!

PLATONOV *stops and turns.*

I knew you wouldn't be asleep. How can anyone sleep on a night like this? God made the winter for sleeping! Come here, Platonov.

PLATONOV (*reluctantly crosses to her*). What are you doing here?

ANNA PETROVNA. Taking a little walk in the moonlight. (*She leads him gently by the arm away from the house.*) What are *you* doing here? You disappeared without so much as a word of goodbye. You didn't think that I should let you get away with such discourtesy?

PLATONOV. I apologise.

ANNA PETROVNA. But what big eyes he has, out here in the moonlight! Don't be frightened — I'm not going to eat you.

PLATONOV. I see you are set upon some foolishness.

ANNA PETROVNA. Foolishness comes with age, Platonov.

PLATONOV. And age excuses it. But you're not old. You're as young as the summer itself. You have your life in front of you.

ANNA PETROVNA. I don't want my life in front of me — I want it now! Because, yes, I am young! It's terrible how young I am! I can feel it stirring in me like the night air among the trees.

PLATONOV. Anna Petrovna, I beg you to think what you're doing.

ANNA PETROVNA. I have thought.

PLATONOV. All your intelligence, all your beauty, all your youth — and you have to come to me! You come bent on conquest, on storming a stronghold. But no great conquest will you have. I know I took a high tone with you before. But I realise, when I look back on my behaviour tonight, that I had no right to such a tone. It's not a stronghold you're attacking — it's a weakhold! Anna Petrovna, you can't rely on my defences!

ANNA PETROVNA. Self-abasement is a form of pride. But what are we to do, Misha? We've got to finish the thing one way or another.

PLATONOV. Finish it? We haven't started it!

ANNA PETROVNA. How can you say that? How can you lie to me, on such a night as this, beneath such a sky? Tell your lies in the autumn, if you must, in the gloom and the mud, but not now, not here. You're being watched! Look up, you absurd man! A thousand eyes, all shining with indignation! You must be good and true, just as all this is good and true. Don't break this silence with your little words!

She takes his hands, and they sit down on the timbers of the crossing, facing each other.

There's no man in the world I could ever love as I love you. There's no woman in the world you could ever love as you love me. Let's take that love; and all the rest, that so torments you — we'll leave that to others to worry about.

PLATONOV (*kisses her hands*). Odysseus was worth the sirens' song, but I'm no Odysseus, you lovely siren of the forest. If only I could give you happiness! But I can't, and I shan't. I shall do what I've done to every woman who has thrown herself at me; I shall make you unhappy!

ANNA PETROVNA. Are you really such a terrible Don Juan? You look so handsome in the moonlight!

PLATONOV. I know myself! The only stories that end happily are the ones that don't have me in them.

ANNA PETROVNA. Such a solemn face! It's a woman who's come to call, not a wild animal! All right — if you really hate it all so much I'll go away again. Is that what you want? I'll go away, and everything will be just as it was before. Yes . . .? (*She laughs.*) Idiot! Take it! Snatch it! Seize it! What more do you want? Smoke it to the end, like a cigarette — pinch it out — tread it under your heel. Be human! (*She gently shakes him.*) You funny creature! A woman who loves you — a woman you love — fine summer weather. What could be simpler than that? (*She lays her head on his knees.*) You don't realise how hard life is for me.

PLATONOV. I shan't make it easier.

ANNA PETROVNA. And yet life is what I long for. Everything is alive, nothing is ever still. We're surrounded by life. We must live, too, Misha! Leave all the problems for tomorrow. Tonight, on this night of nights, we'll simply live!

PLATONOV. Let me make one last appeal. As a man of honour . . .

ANNA PETROVNA (*embraces him*). Don't be stupid, Misha. I'm never going to let you go. You're mine!

PLATONOV. One final plea . . .

ANNA PETROVNA. If I can't do it nicely I'll take you by force! (*She throws her kerchief round his neck.*) Come on!

PLATONOV. It'll end badly.

ANNA PETROVNA. You should write stern editiorials in the newspapers.

PLATONOV. You'll see.

ANNA PETROVNA. You'd be good at that.

PLATONOV. Where are we going, then?

ANNA PETROVNA. To the old summerhouse!

SASHA (*calls sleepily, off*). Misha!

>PLATONOV *and* ANNA PETROVNA *stop.*

PLATONOV. Sasha . . . I'd forgotten all about her.

ANNA PETROVNA. So had I.

PLATONOV. How could I just forget about her?

ANNA PETROVNA. It wouldn't be for the first time.

SASHA (*off*). Misha?

PLATONOV. I'll just get her off to sleep.

ANNA PETROVNA. Platonov!

PLATONOV. I can't leave her wondering where I am!

SASHA (*off*). Where are you, Misha?

ANNA PETROVNA. But that might take another hour!

PLATONOV. Two minutes! She falls asleep like a child if I stroke her head. Wait here!

ANNA PETROVNA. If you're not back in two minutes . . .

PLATONOV. I'll be back!

ANNA PETROVNA. . . . . I'll come in and fetch you!

>*Enter* SASHA *from the house.*

SASHA. Misha?

PLATONOV. Here, my love!

>*Exeunt* PLATONOV *and* SASHA *into the house. Enter* OSIP *from beneath the trees.*

ANNA PETROVNA. Who's that?

OSIP. See that stump there? Rotten. So it glows in the dark. As if a dead man had risen from his grave.

ANNA PETROVNA. Osip . . .

OSIP. My mother used to say that under every stump that glows in the dark there's a sinner buried. That's why the stump glows. To make us pray for his soul. I used to wonder how there could be so many glowing stumps in the forest.

ANNA PETROVNA. How long have you been there, Osip?

OSIP. Long enough.

ANNA PETROVNA. Were you spying?

OSIP. I thought you were some kind of saint.

ANNA PETROVNA. Used you to be in love with me then, Osip?

OSIP. If you'd have told me to walk into the fire, I'd have walked into the fire.

ANNA PETROVNA. You're not still in love with me?

OSIP. That's not my place to say. (*He weeps.*)

ANNA PETROVNA. Oh, and he's crying. Come on, we'll be friends again. You can bring me some more baby hares. Just so long as you promise me one thing . . .

OSIP. If I'd had a gun in my hands as I stood there!

ANNA PETROVNA. One thing, Osip: you won't ever hurt him. Promise?

OSIP. I'll promise this: if he should ever hurt you . . . (*He pulls out his hunting-knife.*)

> *Enter* PLATONOV *from the house.*

PLATONOV. She's asleep!

> OSIP *disappears beneath the trees.*

ANNA PETROVNA. Misha! We must go! Quickly! Before anything else happens!

> *She takes his arm, and they start into the forest.*
> *Enter* DR TRILETZKY, *drunker than before.*

DR TRILETZKY. Who's that? That Sasha? Sasha!

> PLATONOV *returns.* ANNA PETROVNA *remains hidden among the trees.*

PLATONOV. Sh! Sasha's asleep! You'll wake her!

DR TRILETZKY. Oh, it's you. Thought it was Sasha.

PLATONOV. Sasha's asleep.

DR TRILETZKY. Took Porfiry Semyonovich home, you see. Me and Gerasim Kuzmich. Don't like Gerasim Kuzmich, do you, Misha. *I* like him. Wonderful man, Misha. Wonderful drinker. Lost him somewhere . . . Thought I'd just ask Sasha if I could sleep here.

PLATONOV. Well, you can't ask her, because she's asleep.

DR TRILETZKY. She's asleep?

PLATONOV. Fast asleep.

DR TRILETZKY. I'll wake her up.

PLATONOV. Don't wake her up!

DR TRILETZKY. Can't find my way home, Misha.

PLATONOV. Well, you can't stay here.

DR TRILETZKY. Sasha won't mind.

PLATONOV. Sasha's asleep.

DR TRILETZKY. I'll wake her up.

PLATONOV. Don't go in there!

DR TRILETZKY (*calls*). Sasha!

PLATONOV. Listen! Listen! The village storekeeper — he's ill. You've got to go.

> DR TRILETZKY *flaps his hand dismissively.*

It's urgent . . . You've got to operate!

DR TRILETZKY. Operate?

PLATONOV. You know you like operating!

DR TRILETZKY. Can't operate now, Misha! It's the middle of the night! It's past the passenger!

PLATONOV. That wasn't the passenger. That was only the goods.

DR TRILETZKY (*goes towards the house*). Can't operate now. Haven't got my little bag.

PLATONOV (*turns him back towards the village*). Come on. You've got your penknife.

DR TRILETZKY (*heads back towards the house*). Have a little sleep first.

PLATONOV (*turns him round*). Have a little sleep afterwards.

> DR TRILETZKY *begins to go off the way he came.* ANNA PETROVNA *emerges from the shadows, and* PLATONOV *goes to join her.* DR TRILETZKY *turns back towards the house.*

DR TRILETZKY. Think my little bag may be in here.

PLATONOV (*intercepts him*). Have you no shame? Have you no honour?

DR TRILETZKY. Not at one o'clock in the morning, Misha!

PLATONOV. What sort of man are you, Nikolai? What god do you serve? What are you doing with your life? Do you think you were put in this world just to eat and drink and behave like a swine?

DR TRILETZKY. I'm a swine, Misha, you're right.

PLATONOV. What are we all doing with our lives? (*He weeps.*) What god do *I* serve?

DR TRILETZKY. You're crying! Don't cry, Misha!

PLATONOV. What's going to become of us all? Dirt in the ground! That's all we shall ever make!

DR TRILETZKY. All right, Misha. I'll go and open him up.

PLATONOV. We've lost our way, Nikolai! All of us! We're not worth the dust we're made of!

DR TRILETZKY (*weeps*). I'll go, Misha!

PLATONOV. It's all so vile! It's all so foul and threadbare!

DR TRILETZKY. I'm going, Misha, I'm going! Your eyes are sparkling in the moonlight! Shining like green bottle-glass!

> *Exit* DR TRILETZKY *the way he entered.*

ANNA PETROVNA *emerges from the shadows again.*

ANNA PETROVNA. Has he gone?

PLATONOV. Yes, he's gone. Gone to save a human life. And what am *I* doing?

ANNA PETROVNA (*puts an arm round his shoulders*). You're going to save a human life. Your own life!

PLATONOV. It's not me who's coming with you. It's the devil at my back who says 'Go on, go on!' It's not me who obeys him — it's my weak flesh.

ANNA PETROVNA (*moves away from him sharply*). Oh, for heaven's sake! (*She strikes him with her whip.*) If you want to come with me then come with me. If you don't then to hell with it!

   A shot, off, followed by a wild cry of alarm.

He's going to kill you! (*She throws her arms round him protectively.*)

PLATONOV. What? Who? Where?

ANNA PETROVNA. He's fetched a gun! He's going to kill you!

   She drags PLATONOV *into hiding under the trees.*
   Enter VOYNITZEV *and* COLONEL TRILETZKY *from the forest. They are both carrying sporting guns, and are both drunk.*

VOYNITZEV (*sees smoke curling from one of the barrels of his gun*). Was that me?

COLONEL TRILETZKY. My dear chap, another inch and it would have been *me!*

VOYNITZEV. My ears are still ringing!

COLONEL TRILETZKY. I said, you almost shot me!

VOYNITZEV. Great shock to me, too, but don't shout, you'll wake him up. (*He prods* COLONEL TRILETZKY *warningly with his gun.*)

COLONEL TRILETZKY. Yes. Sh! (*He puts the gun to his lips.*)

VOYNITZEV. Sh! (*He does the same.*)

> *They cross to the house.*

COLONEL TRILETZKY. Right outside his window!

VOYNITZEV. Biggest surprise of his life!

COLONEL TRILETZKY. Twenty-one gun salute!

> *They raise their guns to fire. Enter* PLATONOV *from the shadows.*

PLATONOV. No! No!

VOYNITZEV. What the devil . . . ?

> *They level their guns at* PLATONOV.

COLONEL TRILETZKY. Halt! Who goes there!

VOYNITZEV. One more step and we'll shoot!

PLATONOV. It's me! It's me! Platonov! Misha!

VOYNITZEV. Misha?

PLATONOV. Don't shout!

COLONEL TRILETZKY. We're not shouting.

VOYNITZEV. We're shooting.

PLATONOV. Don't shout *or* shoot! You'll wake Sasha!

VOYNITZEV. Oh yes. Sasha.

COLONEL TRILETSKY. My little girl.

VOYNITZEV. Mustn't wake Sasha.

PLATONOV. What are you doing here?

COLONEL TRILETZKY (*to* VOYNITZEV). What are we doing here?

VOYNITZEV (*to* PLATONOV). We're looking for you!

COLONEL TRILETZKY. Show you my new gun!

VOYNITZEV. Give you a surprise!

COLONEL TRILETZKY. Twenty-one gun salute!

VOYNITZEV. Twenty-one gun salute!

They raise their guns to fire.

PLATONOV. *No!*

VOYNITZEV. Sh!

COLONEL TRILETZKY. Sh!

VOYNITZEV. Mustn't wake Sasha.

PLATONOV. Right, now will you get out of here.

VOYNITZEV. We want you to come shooting with us!

PLATONOV. Shooting? It's the middle of the night! It's gone the goods — it's almost the passenger!

COLONEL TRILETZKY. His wife — charming girl . . .

VOYNITZEV. Sofya. You've met Sofya.

COLONEL TRILETZKY. She told me to take him out and shoot him. Take him out and shoot him? — Take him out shooting.

VOYNITZEV. Very difficult to see anything to shoot.

COLONEL TRILETZKY. You could shoot owls, she said.

VOYNITZEV. Very difficult to see owls.

COLONEL TRILETZKY. He's drunk, of course.

VOYNITZEV. First time in my life, Misha! Oh God, I'm so happy! (*He embraces* PLATONOV.)

PLATONOV. Keep that gun away from me, will you?

VOYNITZEV. Oh yes. Mustn't wake Sasha.

COLONEL TRILETZKY. Creep quietly away.

VOYNITZEV. Indians on the warpath. Not a sound.

They begin to stumble away into the forest.

COLONEL TRILETZKY. I know what we can do!

VOYNITZEV. Sh! What?

COLONEL TRILETZKY. Serenade Anna Petrovna! Stand under her window and give her the old artillery serenade!

VOYNITZEV. How does that go?

COLONEL TRILETZKY. The twenty-one gun salute!

VOYNITZEV. Oh, the twenty-one gun salute!

They raise their guns to fire.

PLATONOV. Go away!

VOYNITZEV. Oh yes.

They guiltily place their guns against each other's lips.

COLONEL TRILETZKY. Sh!

VOYNITZEV. Sh!

Exeunt COLONEL TRILETZKY *and* VOYNITZEV *into the forest.*
ANNA PETROVNA *comes out of hiding.*

ANNA PETROVNA. Misha!

PLATONOV. Coming, coming.

SASHA (*off*). Misha?

PLATONOV (*calls*). Coming!

ANNA PETROVNA. Misha, yes or no!

PLATONOV *hesitates.*

PETRIN (*off*). So where is she?

ANNA PETROVNA *looks round to see who this is.*

Who knows? Playing duets with Platonov!

Exit PLATONOV *into the house.*

Out in the woods with the colonel!

ANNA PETROVNA (*to* PLATONOV). We might as well be in the centre of Petersburg!

She sees that PLATONOV *has gone, and goes back into hiding.*

Enter PETRIN, *supported by* DR TRILETZKY. PETRIN *is in his shirtsleeves, and is even drunker than the doctor.*

PETRIN. And where is *he?* He's gone home with a heart attack! What kind of lover is that? Makes an assignation in an old summerhouse, on a moonlit night in June, then lies down and has a heart attack!

DR TRILETZKY. Now you follow the rails, look. Be home in no time. No one around . . . I think I'm just going to have a little sleep at my sister's here.

PETRIN. No one could accuse me of impatience, Kolya!

DR TRILETZKY. Just step to one side when the train comes.

PETRIN. I own that woman! I own the clothes on her back! I own her stepson's underpants! All mine, Kolya! And what do I get in return? I get treated like dirt! Leant across by the servants! Spoken to like a pig!

DR TRILETZKY. Where's your jacket?

PETRIN (*feels in a non-existent breast pocket*). They've taken the money out of my pocket now!

DR TRILETZKY. They've taken the pocket, too, Gerasya!

> PETRIN *starts away up the railway track.*
> DR TRILETZKY *turns towards the house, laughing.*

PETRIN. But thus far, Kolya! Thus far and no further! (*He stumbles over a sleeper and falls down on the track.*)

DR TRILETZKY (*calls, delighted*). Sasha!

Enter PLATONOV *from the house.*

Misha . . . !

PLATONOV. Well?

DR TRILETZKY. It's Gerasim Kuzmich! He's been with the village girls again! Only I've got his money — so they stole his jacket!

PLATONOV. And the storekeeper?

DR TRILETZKY. The storekeeper?

PLATONOV. Have you seen him?

DR TRILETZKY. Saw Gerasim Kuzmich . . .

PLATONOV. He's dying, Kolya!

DR TRILETZKY. He'd fallen into a blackberry bush . . . Yes, well, the storekeeper . . .

> DR TRILETZKY *retreats from* PLATONOV *back in the direction he came from.*

I suppose it doesn't matter if *I* die . . .

> *Exit* DR TRILETZKY.
> *Enter* ANNA PETROVNA *from under the trees.*

ANNA PETROVNA. Platonov! Are you coming with me or not? Because I'm not going back behind that tree.

PLATONOV. All right. All right . . .

ANNA PETROVNA. If it's not your brother-in-law it's your father-in-law. If it's not your father-in-law it's . . .

> *Enter* SASHA *from the house.*

SASHA. Misha! What's happening? What are you doing out here? Is that someone with you? (*She laughs.*) Anna Petrovna!

ANNA PETROVNA. Alexandra Ivanovna.

SASHA. What in the name of goodness are you doing here at this time of night? You're dressed for driving . . . And you're inviting us! Oh, what a lovely idea! It's such a beautiful night! Do let's go, Misha! I'll get dressed!

> *Exit* SASHA *into the house.*

ANNA PETROVNA. So now what are you going to do, Platonov?

PLATONOV. I don't know.

ANNA PETROVNA. Well, I shall be in the old summerhouse. If you want to see me you must come to me there.

PLATONOV. But what shall I tell Sasha?

ANNA PETROVNA. That's your business! I'm not going to lie to your wife for you!

Exit ANNA PETROVNA.

PLATONOV. Anna Petrovna . . . ! (*He turns and goes towards the house.*) Sasha . . . !

Enter DR TRILETZKY.

DR TRILETZKY. And another thing.

PLATONOV. You still haven't gone?

DR TRILETZKY. I'm going! One word of advice first, my friend! If you're going to preach at people then you must preach what you practise!

PLATONOV. Come here! (*He advances on him.*)

DR TRILETZKY (*backs away*). I'm going, I'm going!

PLATONOV. No, you're not. You're not in a fit condition to see a patient. Sasha will have to put you to bed.

DR TRILETZKY. You call *me* a swine, but I don't go around kissing people with whom other people may very well be in . . . Bed? Go to bed?

Enter SASHA, *dressed, from the house.*

SASHA. I've always longed to go for a drive in the moonlight! Where are we going?

PLATONOV. We're not going anywhere. You've got to put your brother to bed.

SASHA. Kolya! Oh, no!

PLATONOV. He can sleep in the classroom.

DR TRILETZKY (*bewildered*). Sleep? Lie down?

PLATONOV. Quickly, now! I think he's going to be sick!

SASHA (*leads* DR TRILETZKY *into the house*). And you'll wake the baby, so then I'll have to get *him* back to sleep.

DR TRILETZKY. Everything's going round. It's all turned back to front!

PLATONOV. I'll tell Anna Petrovna we'll come another time, shall I?

SASHA. Another time, yes, another time.

Exeunt SASHA *and* DR TRILETZKY *into the house.*

PLATONOV (*to himself*): I'm going, then. (*He begins to move irresolutely off.*) It's not as if I were the only man in the world to behave like this . . . (*He falls over* PETRIN.)

PETRIN. They all walk over me.

PLATONOV. Gerasim Kuzmich . . .

PETRIN. Not going to go on walking over me.

PLATONOV. You've been with the village girls again. (*He sits down on the rail beside* PETRIN.) We're all the same. One word from a woman, and that's all we can think of.

PETRIN. One word from me, and up the sign will go! 'To be sold at public auction.'

Enter SOFYA *from the forest, very nervous, her face concealed. She tries to see into the windows of the house.*

PLATONOV. Is that what our lives are going to amount to? One long procession of women?

SOFYA (*taps at the window and whispers desperately*). Misha!

PLATONOV. Sasha! That settles it! I must have been mad! (*He hurries across to* SOFYA.) Here I am, my treasure! I'll never leave you! Not for a moment! Not ever!

SOFYA. Misha! Oh, Misha!

PLATONOV. Sofya!

SOFYA (*throws herself into his arms*). I waited for you after the fireworks! Waited and waited! I was sure you'd come! I made my husband go out shooting with the colonel — they're both drunk — they'll shoot each other — I must be mad! You said you would, Misha! You promised you would!

PLATONOV. Would what?

SOFYA. Uproot us both!

PLATONOV. Oh yes.

SOFYA. Uproot me, Misha!

PLATONOV. Yes, but not here!

SASHA opens the window of the house.

SASHA. Misha . . .

PLATONOV (*to* SOFYA, *warningly*). Sasha!

SASHA. Was that you tapping on the window?

PLATONOV (*to* SASHA): No? (*To* SOFYA:) In the old summer-house! (*To* SASHA:) Yes! Only me! (*To* SOFYA:) No!

SASHA. No?

PLATONOV (*to* SASHA): Yes! (*To* SOFYA:) Not in the old summerhouse!

SASHA. What?

PLATONOV (*to* SASHA): Nothing! (*To* SOFYA:) In the new summerhouse!

Exit SOFYA *into the forest.*

SASHA. I can't understand a word.

SASHA closes the window. PLATONOV *pulls* PETRIN *up into a sitting position.*

PLATONOV. Gerasya! Help me! What am I going to do? Which way, Gerasya? Which one — old or new?

There is the sound of a distant train whistle, and a tiny star of light appears on the horizon at the end of the railway track.

Train . . . ! Yes! I'll run to the station! Go away, and never come back . . . !

PETRIN. Never get her married to him now.

PLATONOV. But she is, isn't she? She's in love with me, too!

PETRIN. I'll take her to court.

PLATONOV. So this is happiness, then. This is what it feels like . . .

PETRIN. And up the sign will go.

PLATONOV. But where, Gerasya? Which? And just a moment — which is where . . . ?

Enter SASHA *from the house.*

SASHA. Misha! Where are you! What's all this about a summer-house?

PLATONOV *drops* PETRIN *back on to the track, and flees in the direction taken by* ANNA PETROVNA. *But he meets* OSIP *emerging from beneath the trees, and diverts to go off in the direction taken by* SOFYA.

Osip! What's happening? I don't understand . . . Osip, what are you doing?

OSIP *lies down across the level crossing. The headlight of the approaching train grows slowly bigger.*

You can't lie there! Osip, get up! The train's coming!

OSIP (*sobs*). He's gone to her! Gone to Anna Petrovna! And she loves him! She loves him!

SASHA. You're lying.

OSIP. God strike me down — I heard every word!

SASHA. He's left me, then! He's left me! Kill me, Lord! Mother of God, kill me!

The whistle of the approaching train. SASHA *runs towards it with outstretched arms.* OSIP *jumps up and runs after her.*

OSIP. No! No!

They stumble over PETRIN, *who sits up. They stop and turn round to gaze at him in astonishment.*

PETRIN. Yes! Yes! You'll see! Tomorrow!

SASHA *and* OSIP *drag* PETRIN *clear of the track as the headlight widens, and the roar of the approaching train and*

*the scream of the whistle rise to a crescendo. The outer
wall of the schoolhouse is turned and trucked across the
railway line, hiding the scene, as the lights go down. The
roar of the train and the scream of the whistle continue
through the auditorium in the darkness, until the lights
come up for:-*

Scene Two

The PLATONOVs' *living-room inside the schoolhouse. The
wooden baulks of the level crossing now form the rough timber
floor of the room. In the rear wall of the room are a window and
a door; beyond it are the same tall trees of the forest as in the
earlier scenes. There is a sofa in the room, a cupboard, a table
with two chairs, and all the signs of a cramped, muddled and
sleazy life. It is early evening. The sound of the train continues as
the lights come up — quietly now, going away in the distance.*

PLATONOV *is lying on the sofa, fast asleep, with a straw hat
covering his face.*

Enter SOFYA.

SOFYA. Platonov! Wake up! (*She shakes him.*) Misha! (*She takes
the hat off his face.*) How could you put this filthy object on
your face! Ugh! What a mess you are! Haven't washed, have
you? Lying here in your dirty undershirt — all the hair on your
chest displayed to the world . . . And look at this pig-sty! It's
only three weeks since your wife walked out. It would break
her heart if she could see it now . . . Misha, I'm talking to you!
Get up!

PLATONOV. Um?

SOFYA. Wake up, will you!

PLATONOV. Just a minute.

SOFYA. Now!

PLATONOV (*sits up*). Oh, it's you.

SOFYA. Yes, it's me! (*She holds her watch in front of his eyes.*) Look!

PLATONOV. Right. (*He lies down again.*)

SOFYA. Platonov!

PLATONOV. What do you want? (*He sits up.*) What is it?

SOFYA. Look at the time!

PLATONOV. Fussing away again, are you, Sofya?

SOFYA. Yes, I'm fussing away again! Look at this watch, will you! Now tell me what it says.

PLATONOV. Five-and-twenty to seven.

SOFYA. Five-and-twenty to seven, yes. Have you forgotten what we agreed?

PLATONOV. What did we agree? Don't talk in riddles, please. I'm not up to it today.

SOFYA. You have forgotten. What's the matter with you? Your eyes are red. You look as if you've been crumpled up into a ball and thrown away . . . You're not ill, are you . . . ? What we agreed was to meet at the usual place. At six o'clock.

PLATONOV. Go on.

SOFYA. What do you mean, Go on? Aren't you ashamed of yourself? You gave me your word of honour! (*She sits beside him.*)

PLATONOV. I'd have kept it, too, if I hadn't fallen asleep. You could see for yourself — I was fast asleep! I don't know what you're going on about.

SOFYA. Have you been on time for a single one of our meetings? Every day you give me your word of honour — and every day you break it!

PLATONOV. Well, this is all very charming.

SOFYA. Why do you stop being high-minded and intelligent when you're with me? I owe my spiritual salvation to you!

Why do you stop being yourself? You behave like some kind of monster whenever I'm with you. Never a kind look or a kind word — never a mention of love. I come to you — and you smell of drink, you're dressed all anyhow, and you plainly haven't put a comb through your hair. And if I say anything you snap back at me and change the subject.

PLATONOV (*jumps up, and walks up and down the room*). So, here you are.

SOFYA. Are you drunk?

PLATONOV. None of your business.

SOFYA. And that's very charming, I must say! (*She weeps.*)

PLATONOV. Women!

SOFYA. And don't start saying 'Women'! If I've heard it once I've heard it a thousand times! I'm sick of it! What are you doing to me? You're making me ill! Can't you see that? You hate me, don't you! Are you trying to kill me? Well, I'm not some poor simple village girl, and I'm not going to let myself be humiliated like this. (*She weeps.*) My God! My God!

PLATONOV. Now that's enough.

SOFYA. It's barely three weeks since . . . Since that night! And already I'm only a shadow of myself! Where's the happiness you promised me? And where's all this going to end? Think, if you're so clever! Start thinking now, before it's too late! Sit down right here on this chair, clear everything else out of your head, and just think about this one single thing: what are you doing to me?

PLATONOV. I can't think. I've forgotten how to think. You think yourself! All your unhappiness comes from this irregular liaison!

SOFYA. I give myself to him, and he has the nerve to talk about an 'irregular liaison'!

PLATONOV. Oh, come on! We can't start quibbling over every word! You see our relationship one way — I see it another.

I've ruined you; and that's all there is to say about it! And you're not the only one! Wait until your husband finds out!

SOFYA. You're afraid he's going to kill you?

PLATONOV. No. I'm afraid it's going to kill him.

SOFYA. Why did you ever come to me, then? You miserable coward!

PLATONOV. No, please, not the low thrilling tones! They won't make any impression on me. Nor will bursting into tears. Every time we talk you weep!

SOFYA. Yes! And I never wept at all before! Anyway, if you're afraid of killing him you'd better start biting your nails now. He already knows!

PLATONOV. What?

SOFYA. Yes! I told him this afternoon.

PLATONOV. You're not serious!

SOFYA. Look at you. You're as white as a sheet. I don't know why I should love you. I must be mad!

PLATONOV. How did he take it?

SOFYA. Just like you. He was afraid. His skin went grey. He started to cry. Then he crumpled up. He went down and crawled on all fours . . . And he had just the same repellent look on his face as you have now.

PLATONOV. You've killed him! Do you realise that? How could you sit there and tell me it all so calmly? You've killed him! Did you . . . did you say it was me?

SOFYA. Of course. What else could I have done?

PLATONOV. How could you say the words?

SOFYA. Platonov! Have some shame! You mean I shouldn't have told him?

PLATONOV. Of course you shouldn't have told him! You shouldn't have told him anything! (*He sinks to his knees*

and puts his head down on the sofa.) Cried! Crawled on all
fours! Oh, that poor wretched man! If you hadn't told him
he'd have gone to his grave without ever finding out!

SOFYA. I had to tell him! I do have some self-respect!

PLATONOV. You know what you've done, don't you? You've
parted forever.

SOFYA. Forever, yes. What alternative did I have?

PLATONOV. But what's going to happen to you when *we* part?
Because part we very soon shall! You'll be the first to shake
off the spell. You'll be the first to open your eyes. And then
you'll leave me! (*He flaps his hand.*) Well, you do whatever
you think best. You're a better person than I am. You've got
a cleverer head on your shoulders. You take the whole mess
over! Just tell me what to do! Get me up on my feet again, if
you have the power. And do it now, for the love of God,
before I go out of my mind!

SOFYA. We'll leave tonight.

PLATONOV. The sooner the better.

SOFYA. I wrote to my mother about you. We'll go to her.

PLATONOV. Anywhere you like! Just as long as we get away
from here!

SOFYA. Misha! This will be our new life, though! Do you see?
Trust me, love! I'll get you up on your feet again! I'll take
you somewhere lighter and brighter — somewhere free of
dirt and lethargy — somewhere where there's no lying around
in filthy undershirts. I'll make a man of you. I'll give you
happiness. I'll make you work! We'll be proper people, Misha!
We'll eat our bread in the sweat of our faces. We'll harden our
hands. (*She lays her head on his chest.*) I'll work, too.

PLATONOV. What do you know about work?

SOFYA. Trust me, Misha, that's all you have to do! You raised
me from the dead, and all my life will be a thank-offering for
that. We'll leave tonight, then, on the evening train. Yes? I'll

go and get ready at once. You get your things together. We'll meet at the usual place an hour from now. Let's say quarter to eight. Yes? You will be there?

PLATONOV. I shall be there.

SOFYA. Word of honour?

PLATONOV. I said — I shall be there!

SOFYA. Give me your word of honour.

PLATONOV. Word of honour.

SOFYA. I don't want to have to come looking for you again . . . Cheer up, then! (*She kisses him.*) We're going to start our lives afresh, Misha! By tomorrow you'll be a different man! We'll be breathing new air! We'll have new blood flowing in our veins!

PLATONOV. Of course we will . . . Did you say quarter past eight or quarter past nine?

SOFYA. Quarter to eight! Or we'll miss the train! I've got some money — we'll eat on the way. (*She laughs.*) And smarten yourself up a bit for the journey!

    SOFYA *runs out of the house.*

PLATONOV (*to himself*). A new life! That's an old song! I've heard that one a few times! (*Pause.*) I'd better write to him. And to Sasha. They can have a little weep, and then they can forgive and forget. So it's goodbye to everyone, because tomorrow I'm going to be a different man! (*He opens the cupboard.*) What am I going to put my clean underwear in? I haven't got a suitcase . . . (*He takes one of the many bottles in the cupboard and pours himself a drink.*) Goodbye, old school of mine! Goodbye, boys and girls! (*He drinks.*) Your kindly old teacher, the swine, is doing a bolt . . . Was that me drinking? What am I drinking for? I'm giving up drinking! Well, this is the last drink I shall ever have . . . So, sit down and write to Sasha . . . (*He lies down on the sofa.*) Sofya really does believe it all, doesn't she . . . Well, blessed are they that have faith . . .

As long as she hasn't told Anna Petrovna . . . Letter from Anna Petrovna somewhere . . . (*He reaches up and pulls an unopened envelope off a shelf, which brings a whole avalanche of mostly unopened letters down on top of him.*) Hundreds of letters from her! She hasn't stopped writing, ever since that wild and crazy night . . . (*He opens the letter absently.*) Neat, bold hand she's got . . . Just so long as I don't have to come face to face with her! She'd get the truth out of me in . . . (*He reads.*) 'If you don't answer this one, either, I shall come round there and . . .'

> *A knock at the door.* PLATONOV *jumps up in alarm, then stands undecided. Another knock. He goes quietly to the window, and opens it to climb out. Then he sees the glass of vodka still standing by the sofa, and goes back to conceal it in the cupboard. Another knock — but now he has noticed the pile of letters. He picks them up to hide them, and the door begins to open cautiously.* PLATONOV *conceals himself behind it.*

> *Enter, cautiously,* MARKO, *with his satchel.*

MARKO. Anyone at home?

PLATONOV. Who's this?

MARKO. Me, sir. That you, sir?

PLATONOV (*cautiously*). Yes?

MARKO. Platonov?

PLATONOV. What of it?

MARKO. Mikhail Vasilyevich Platonov?

PLATONOV. What do you want?

MARKO. From the magistrate, sir! (*He hands an envelope round the door to* PLATONOV.)

PLATONOV (*emerges from hiding, relieved*). From the magistrate? Oh . . . not *another* christening! (*He opens the envelope.*) Breeds like a rabbit, that man! (*He reads.*) 'You are hereby summoned . . .' (*To* MARKO.) Do you know what you look like, cowering away behind the door there?

MARKO. Yes, sir.

PLATONOV. Oh, you know, do you?

MARKO. Yes, sir.

PLATONOV (*reads*). 'You are hereby summoned to appear before His Imperial Majesty's Justice of the Peace . . .' (*To* MARKO.) What do you look like, then?

MARKO. Like God, sir.

PLATONOV. Like God?

MARKO. Made in the image and likeness, sir.

PLATONOV. Oh yes. (*He reads.*) '. . . before His Imperial Majesty's Justice of the Peace to answer a charge of indecent assault . . .' It's not an invitation!

MARKO. No, sir.

PLATONOV. It's a summons!

MARKO. Yes, sir.

PLATONOV (*reads*). ' . . . a charge of indecent assault, which charge has been laid upon the complaint of Marya Yefimovna Grekova . . .'! (*He laughs.*) Well, dash me! Good old Beetle-juice! I didn't know she'd got it in her!

MARKO. Sign for it, then, will you, sir? Just here, sir.

PLATONOV (*signs*). When's the case being heard . . . ? The day after tomorrow. I'll be there! She should have done this last summer!

MARKO. Thank you, sir. (*He holds out his hand.*) Drink your health, sir.

PLATONOV. You can drink it in tea. (*He takes the tea-caddy out of the cupboard.*) Where do you want it?

> MARKO *holds his pocket open.* PLATONOV *pours the tea straight in.*

What a little champion she is, though! Never expected that! Who have they got as witnesses?

MARKO (*sorts through the subpoenas in his bag*). 'Dr Nikolai Ivanovich Triletzky.'

PLATONOV. The doctor? He'll be a comic turn! Who else?

MARKO. 'Sofya Yegorovna Voynitzeva.'

PLATONOV. Sofya Yegorovna? She won't be there! She's going away . . . Oh . . . Oh, yes . . . Take Marya Yefimovna a message will you?

MARKO. Marya Yefimovna — message. Yes?

PLATONOV. Tell her I'm very sorry . . .

MARKO. Very sorry.

PLATONOV. But I can't accept her kind summons because I'm going away.

MARKO. Going away.

PLATONOV. Forever, tell her.

MARKO. Going away forever. Right.

PLATONOV. Say I behaved like a swine, but then I've behaved like a swine with everybody. Say I should have been happy to kiss her again, with proper respect, before the whole world in open court.

MARKO. Like a swine. In open court.

PLATONOV. All right. Do you know where she lives?

MARKO. Good seven miles from here, sir. (*He holds out his hand.*) Can't walk seven miles on a glass of tea, sir!

PLATONOV. All right — a ruble. A ruble there, a ruble back, and a ruble for remembering it. Three rubles when you get back here and tell me you've delivered it! Off you go, then. Oh, and Marko . . .

MARKO. Yes, sir?

PLATONOV. That's what God looks like, is it?

MARKO. So I humbly believe, sir.

Exit MARKO.

PLATONOV (*to himself*). First time in my life I've ever been brought to book by a woman! Usually you treat them like dirt, and what do they do? — They hang around your neck . . . Oh, yes — Sasha. I was writing to Sasha . . . (*He finds the heap of unopened letters.*) No, I wasn't. I was hiding these before Anna Petrovna . . .

> *A sharp knock at the door. He gazes at the door, transfixed, then tries to stuff the letters away inside the cupboard. The door is flung open, and* OSIP *enters. The letters come sliding out of the cupboard again.*

(*Over his shoulder.*) Anna Petrovna! This is a surprise. (*He turns and sees* OSIP.) Oh, it's you. What do you want?

> OSIP *sits down.*

What's the matter with you? You look as if you'd been through all the ten plagues of Egypt. I feel as if I'd been through nine of them. You're nothing but skin and bone, though. Are you ill? What are you doing here?

OSIP. Saying goodbye.

PLATONOV. Why? Are you going away?

OSIP. Not me. You.

PLATONOV. Good God, so I am! But how do you know that?

OSIP. I just do.

PLATONOV. Clairvoyant, are you, Osip, on top of all your other skills?

OSIP. I know something else, too. I know where you're going.

PLATONOV. Do you indeed! That's more than I know! Well, this is something that interests me. Where *am* I going?

OSIP. You're going to hell.

PLATONOV. I see. Quite a journey. You're not planning to be

the driver of the train that takes me there, by any chance?

OSIP (*takes out his hunting knife*). I used to have a lot of respect for you. Thought you were the great man ... I've watched you these past weeks, though, you see. Slipping off into the forest at all hours of the day and night ... Well, that's no business of mine, who the general's widow meets on her rides through the forest. But I saw something else tonight. I saw the young mistress come running down here. And I waited. And I saw her go running back again. So then I went and fetched my knife. Because I reckon you're making a fool of the general's widow, and I'm not having that. (*He stands up and seizes* PLATONOV*'s arm.*)

PLATONOV. No! No! I've got a family! I've got a wife and child to support!

OSIP. Where is she, then, your wife? Is she still in the land of the living? I reckon you don't know yourself which of the three's the real one! (*He raises the knife.*)

Enter SASHA *through the front door.*

SASHA (*screams*). Misha! No! No! (*She tries to protect* PLATONOV.) Don't hurt him! Don't touch him!

OSIP (*backs away*). Oh, it's you. You're still around, are you.

SASHA. Give me the knife!

OSIP (*throws it down*). Can't kill him in front of you ... Anyway, you're back ... I *will* kill him, though! He won't ever get away from me!

Exit OSIP.

SASHA. Are you all right?

PLATONOV. Oh, my arm! He twisted my arm! (*He sits down on the sofa.*)

SASHA. Lie down. Put the cushion under your head. (*She settles the cushion for him.*)

PLATONOV. Don't fuss, my pet. I'm perfectly all right.

SASHA. Where does it hurt?

PLATONOV. I'm all right! Don't worry . . . He was going to kill me! He was! He was going to kill me! You were only just in time, Sasha! Another minute and you'd have been a widow! (*He kisses her hand.*) Oh, Sasha! Oh, my treasure . . . ! Are you at your father's ? How is he?

SASHA. He's all right . . . Misha, it's little Vova. That's why I came. He's ill, poor mite. He's got a bad cough, and a rash, and he's running a terrible fever. He won't eat or drink. The last two nights he's just cried all night. (*She weeps.*) Oh, Misha, I'm so worried! What am I going to do? If he died, Misha . . . What would become of us then?

PLATONOV. Yes . . . But God won't take our little boy away from you, Sasha. Why should he punish you? Look after him, Sasha, and I swear to you I'll make a man of him. I haven't been much of a man myself, I know, but as a father I shall be mighty! Oh, my arm! He hasn't broken something, has he . . . ? Don't cry, love! (*He pulls her head down on to his chest.*) You're home again. Why did you ever leave? I love you, lass! I love you deeply! My sins are black, I know, but what can we do? You'll just have to forgive me, won't you?

SASHA. Is the affair over, then?

PLATONOV. The affair . . . What a word to choose!

SASHA. Or isn't it over?

PLATONOV. What can I say? There never was an affair. It's just some kind of absurd nonsense. You should never have let yourself be upset by it. And if it's not over yet then it soon will be!

SASHA. When?

PLATONOV. Sooner rather than later, I should imagine. It won't be long before we're living like we did before, Sasha! Be as sceptical as I am about this thing lasting! Sofya isn't the one for me. The ferment hasn't quite died down in her yet, but, believe me, Sofya won't be your rival for long . . . Sasha, what's the matter?

SASHA. Sofya? It's *Sofya* that you're having an affair with?

PLATONOV. You didn't know?

SASHA. Sofya? But that's terrible!

PLATONOV. Sasha, don't torment me any more! I'm in agony with my arm as it is! Why did you leave me, then? You mean, it wasn't because of Sofya?

SASHA. I thought it was Anna Petrovna! That was bad enough! But another man's wife! That's vile, Misha, that's wicked! I should never have thought it of you! Well, God give you happiness, the pair of you! (*She goes to the door.*)

PLATONOV. Don't talk like that, Sasha! I don't want happiness! Don't go, Sasha! (*He goes after her.*) Don't leave me! Could you truly never forgive me?

SASHA. Could you ever forgive yourself?

PLATONOV. That's an interesting question. (*He kisses her head.*) You don't have to go. I am truly penitent. And if you're not here it's going to be a dismal progression of vodka and squalor and men trying to murder me. I've gone through torment, Sasha! If you won't stay as a wife, then stay as a nurse! You're a strange lot, you know, you women. You feed that good-for-nothing Osip, you kill all the local cats and dogs with kindness, you sit up half the night reciting prayers for your enemies . . . What would it cost you to throw a crust to your own guilty but penitent husband? Why must you be one of the lynch mob? Stay with me, Sasha! (*He embraces her.*) I can't manage without a nursemaid. All right, I've stolen my friend's wife — I'm Sofya's lover — and for all I know I may yet be Anna Petrovna's, too. You've every right to be indignant! But who will ever love you as I love you? Who will you cook dinner for? Who will you oversalt the soup for? You'd be absolutely within your rights to leave me. Nothing could be more richly deserved, But . . . (*He picks her up.*) . . . who's going to pick you up and carry you? How will you ever live without me?

SASHA. Put me down! My life is destroyed, and all you can do is joke about it! (*She gets away from him.*) You must know it's not a joke! How can I live without you? — How could I possibly live *with* you? (*She sobs.*)

PLATONOV. Off you go, then. And God go with you. (*He kisses her on the head, then lies down on the sofa again.*) I do understand.

SASHA. You've broken up our family. We were so happy and peaceful! There was no one on earth as happy as I was. What have you done, Misha? You'll never turn back now . . . Don't come and visit us. Father will bring Vova to see you . . .

> *She looks at him for a moment, then round the room, then goes out.*

PLATONOV (*to himself*). Well, there's someone who's starting a new life . . . Oh, but my God, the pain of it, the pain . . . Poor little Sasha! She's a saint! She's got every right to throw the first stone . . . What was I doing? (*He takes a drink.*) I was going to write to Sasha . . . No, I was going to . . . keep Anna Petrovna out! (*He hurries to the front door and bolts it.*)

> ANNA PETROVNA *appears at the window.*

ANNA PETROVNA. Are you alone?

> PLATONOV *spins guiltily round.*

What are you doing? Don't you recognise me? Have you forgotten who I am?

PLATONOV. Anna Petrovna . . .

> *He crosses to the window, but* ANNA PETROVNA *has disappeared.*

(*To himself:*) Quick! Before she comes back!

> *He hurries to the front door, unbolts it, and opens it to escape. In walks* ANNA PETROVNA. PLATONOV *retreats in front of her.*

ANNA PETROVNA (*reproachfully*). Platonov!

PLATONOV. Anna Petrovna . . .

ANNA PETROVNA. Come here, Platonov. Why are you running away from me?

> PLATONOV *attempts to stuff the letters into the cupboard behind his back.*

Never mind that. It's too late now to start tidying up. Come here!

> PLATONOV *goes over to her. She gives him her hand.*

Why won't you look at me, Platonov?

PLATONOV. I'm ashamed of myself. (*He kisses her hand.*)

ANNA PETROVNA. What are you ashamed about?

PLATONOV. Everything.

ANNA PETROVNA. I see. You've seduced some poor girl, have you?

PLATONOV. Something like that.

ANNA PETROVNA. What are we going to do with you, Platonov? Who is it?

PLATONOV. You don't know?

ANNA PETROVNA. I'm asking you.

PLATONOV. I can't tell you.

ANNA PETROVNA. Perhaps we should sit down.

> *They sit down on the sofa.*

Well, we shall find out who it is, young man, we shall find out. Why do you have to put on this hangdog performance in front of me, though? I know your black heart of old.

PLATONOV. Don't ask me, Anna Petrovna! Talk, by all means, but no questions. I'm not up to being cross-examined today.

ANNA PETROVNA. Very well. Didn't you get my letters?

PLATONOV. Yes.

ANNA PETROVNA. So why didn't you come and see us?

PLATONOV. I couldn't.

ANNA PETROVNA. Why ever not?

PLATONOV. You're asking questions . . . ! I just couldn't.

ANNA PETROVNA. You knew we needed you. Sergey and
    Sofya are behaving very badly. Terrible sulks and silences.
    You wouldn't think they were still on their honeymoon. And
    all because we didn't have our clever fool there to entertain
    us . . . Or didn't you read my letters?

PLATONOV. Of course I read them.

ANNA PETROVNA. So you knew I was waiting for you. You
    knew I was coming here today if you didn't answer.

PLATONOV. I couldn't answer.

ANNA PETROVNA. Sit up straight . . . Anyone would think you
    were ashamed of what happened that night.

PLATONOV. I've been ill.

ANNA PETROVNA. You're lying.

PLATONOV. I'm lying. There's no point in asking me anything.

ANNA PETROVNA. You reek of alcohol. And you look like
    nothing on this earth. Red eyes, terrible complexion. You're
    filthy, the house is filthy . . . Look at it! What sort of mess is
    this? You're drinking, are you?

PLATONOV (*spreads his hands helplessly*). It's the holidays.

ANNA PETROVNA. It's the same story as last summer, isn't it.
    You seduced that wretched girl, and then all the way through
    until the autumn you went round looking like a wet hen.
    Which is what you look like now. A bold Don Juan and a
    miserable coward inhabiting one and the same body. How dare
    you start drinking!

PLATONOV. I'll stop, I'll stop.

ANNA PETROVNA. Word of honour?

PLATONOV. Word of honour.

ANNA PETROVNA. On second thoughts I won't put you to the

trouble of keeping your word. Where's the drink?

PLATONOV *indicates the cupboard.*

You ought to be ashamed of yourself! Have you no character at all? Look at the mess in this cupboard! (*She finds the letters.*) I see. No wonder they had so little effect on you . . . Look at it all, though! Your wife's going to having something to say when she comes back! You do want her back, don't you?

PLATONOV. All I want is for you to stop asking me questions! And to stop trying to make me look you in the eye!

ANNA PETROVNA. Which bottle is the drink in?

PLATONOV. All of them.

ANNA PETROVNA. All of them? It's like a distillery in here! We'll have to get your wife back. You'll just have to make it up with her as best you can . . . It was no part of my plans to get you divorced. I'm not such a terrible rival. I don't mind sharing you . . . Now, I'm going to empty all this foul stuff out of the window. Some vile backyard brew, is it . . . ? (*She pours a little into a glass and tastes it.*) No, it isn't — it's good vodka! All right, then, we'll drink a glass of it first, shall we? Yes? Just a drop to wish it goodbye. Here . . Make the most of it. That's all you're getting. And a drop for me . . . To the wicked of this world! Of whom you're one . . . ! Not at all bad, this vodka. You have a little discrimination, at any rate . . . All right. (*She hands him bottles to carry.*) Out it goes . . . Pity to waste it all, though . . . One more drink first, yes?

PLATONOV. If you like.

ANNA PETROVNA (*pours*). The quicker we drink it the sooner it will be gone.

PLATONOV (*raises his glass*). Sobriety!

ANNA PETROVNA. Sobriety!

They drink.

Didn't you miss me, Platonov . . . ? Why don't we sit down?

Put the bottles on the floor for the moment . . . Did you miss me?

PLATONOV. Every minute of every day.

ANNA PETROVNA. Then why didn't you come and see me?

PLATONOV. I'm dying, my dear, I'm dying! Dying of guilt and melancholy! I'm a soul in torment! Then you arrive, and what happens? — I feel a little better.

ANNA PETROVNA. You've got so thin! What are you doing to yourself? Are you pretending to be the hero of some novel? Doom and gloom in three volumes? If there's one thing I can't stand it's romantic heroes! Why can't you be like other people, you silly man? Why do you always have to be some kind of fallen archangel?

PLATONOV. My dear, what can I do?

ANNA PETROVNA. What can you do? You can stop drinking. You can stop lying here all day. You can wash a little more often. And you can come and see me. (*She gets to her feet.*) Come on! Let's go up to my house now!

PLATONOV. Go to your house? No, no!

ANNA PETROVNA. Yes, come on! Come and talk to Sergey and Sofya! Come and pick a few quarrels!

PLATONOV. No, no, no!

ANNA PETROVNA. Why on earth not?

PLATONOV. I can't.

ANNA PETROVNA. Of course you can! Come on — put your hat on!

PLATONOV. I'm not setting foot outside this house!

ANNA PETROVNA (*puts his hat on his head*). Don't be idiotic! (*She takes him by the arm.*) Now, then. Left, right . . . ! Come on, Platonov! Quick march . . . ! Oh, really, Misha!

PLATONOV. I'm not going.

ANNA PETROVNA. It's like dragging a mule through a gate. Be reasonable, now, Misha! Be nice to me!

PLATONOV. I'm not going!

ANNA PETROVNA. Just for a little walk round the school, then.

PLATONOV. Why keep on about it? I want to stay at home, and that's that!

ANNA PETROVNA. I see. Listen, Platonov . . . Sit down . . .

    They both sit.

Do you know what's happening today? Porfiry Semyonovich is taking the train into town, and tomorrow he's going to buy the estate. He's going to settle all our debts. So I shall have money, Platonov, and I'm going to lend you some, and you're going to go away somewhere for a month or two.

PLATONOV. Go away? Where to?

ANNA PETROVNA. Moscow . . . Petersburg . . . Wherever you like! All right? Do go, Misha. You absolutely must get away from here. Get out and about, see people, go to the theatre, have a complete change. As soon as I get the money from Porfiry Semyonovich. And once the estate is sold *I* shan't have to be here. If you like, love, I'll come with you. Would you like that? We'll take drives together, we'll go for long walks. By the time we get back we shall be quite different people!

PLATONOV. It's a delightful idea. But, alas, impossible. I *am* going away, Anna Petrovna. I'm going tonight. But not with you.

ANNA PETROVNA. Well, please yourself . . . Where are you going?

PLATONOV. Away. (*Pause.*) Forever.

ANNA PETROVNA. Oh, nonsense! (*She drinks.*) Rubbish!

PLATONOV. It's not nonsense, my dear. I am going! And it will be forever!

ANNA PETROVNA. But whatever for? You funny man.

PLATONOV. Don't ask me! But this is the last time we shall see each other. Forget this fool. Forget the blackguard that was Platonov. He's going to disappear off the face of the earth! Perhaps we shall meet again many years from now, when we're both old — old enough to laugh together and shed an ancient tear or two over the past. As the present will mercifully have become. But in the meantime — forget him. (*He kisses her hand.*)

ANNA PETROVNA. Come on, drink up! (*She pours.*) It's no sin to talk nonsense if you're drunk.

PLATONOV (*drinks*). Yes, you can laugh at me. I'm running away from myself. Running away to a new life — and I know only too well what that new life will be like.

ANNA PETROVNA. But what's happened to you?

PLATONOV. You'll find out soon enough. But in your horror when you do, try not to curse me. I shall have been punished already by my separation from you.

ANNA PETROVNA (*through her tears*). I can't think you've done anything so very terrible ... And you'll never survive without me ... I'm a little tiny bit drunk ... We'll go away together.

PLATONOV. No. You'll know why not tomorrow.

ANNA PETROVNA. Stay here, then, love! We could all live so happily! The estate's being sold, I know. But Porfiry Semyonovich is going to buy it — he's in love with me — everything will be all right.

PLATONOV. Just leave me, my dear. Just say goodbye and leave me.

ANNA PETROVNA. One more for old times' sake?

PLATONOV. All right.

ANNA PETROVNA (*pours*). Drink, my love. Drink and to hell with it!

PLATONOV (*drinks*). Be happy! Just go on quietly living here, and never mind about me.

ANNA PETROVNA. If we're going to drink let's drink. (*She pours.*) You die if you drink. But then you die if you don't drink. (*She drinks.*) I'm one, too, Platonov. I'm a drinker . . . Another glass? No, I mustn't, or the words will go. Then what shall I have left? Oh, Misha, it's terrible to be an educated woman. An educated woman with nothing to do. What am I here for? Why am I alive? (*Pause.*) I've no choice but to be immoral. Because I *am* immoral, Platonov. I'm a loose woman. (*She laughs.*) Aren't I? Maybe that's the only reason I love you, because I'm loose. I shall founder, too. People like me always do . . . They should make me a professor somewhere, or a director of something . . . If I were a diplomat I'd turn the whole world upside down . . . An educated woman . . . And nothing to do. So I'm no use. Horses, cows, dogs — they all have their uses. Not me, though. I'm irrelevant . . . Aren't I? Why aren't you saying anything?

PLATONOV. We're both in sorry case.

ANNA PETROVNA. If only I had children . . . Do you like children? Stay here, love! We could all live so happily together! All be friends! You go away, and what will become of me . . . ? I so long to rest, I so much need to rest . . . and at the same time I want to be a wife, I want to be a mother . . . Won't you stay? You do . . . love me, don't you? You funny man. Don't you?

PLATONOV. How could any mortal man not love you?

ANNA PETROVNA. You love me — I love you; what more do you want . . . ? Why didn't you come to me that night . . . ? That wild night . . . Such a strange month it's been. Their honeymoon month. A sort of honeymoon for all of us. A month of wild honey.

PLATONOV. Please go now. If you stay I shall tell you everything, and if I tell you I shall kill myself. (*He takes her to the door.*) Goodbye. Be happy. (*He embraces and kisses her.*) We shall never see each other again.

ANNA PETROVNA. That depends upon whether I can catch him at the station.

PLATONOV. Catch him? Catch whom?

ANNA PETROVNA. Porfiry Semyonovich. He's getting the evening train. He'll have money in his pocket. That's all we need, my love!

Exit ANNA PETROVNA.

PLATONOV (*to himself*). If only we could have gone away together! What would it have been? A few weeks. No more. What's that out of a whole lifetime? I could have seen Moscow again ... I suppose I could ask Sofya to postpone our departure ... We're going to spend the rest of our lives together — she could scarcely object to waiting for a week or two. She could go and stay with her mother — she needs to have a rest and get her strength back ... Just make sure that Anna Petrovna doesn't run into Sergey first!

PLATONOV *opens the front door to run after* ANNA PETROVNA. *There on the doorstep, hand upraised to knock, stands* VOYNITZEV. PLATONOV *falls back, abashed, and retires to the far side of the room.*

VOYNITZEV. One gift and one gift only did God bestow upon me in this life. One precious gift. And then he took it away from me again.

PLATONOV *sits down at the table, and hides his head in his hands.*

What am I? I'm nothing. I'm not very clever. I'm no great figure of a man ... Whereas you have everything. Intelligence, looks, spirit. But they weren't enough for you. You had to have the one thing I possessed — my happiness.

He sits at the table opposite PLATONOV, *and breaks down.*

Give her back to me, Platonov! You've so much fortune in your life! So much happiness! Give her back to me!

PLATONOV. If I had a gun I'd shoot myself.

VOYNITZEV (*laughs through his tears*). That's what I came here for! To challenge you! Or even . . . God forgive me, I don't know what I was going to do! (*He takes a revolver out of his pocket and tosses it down on the table between them.*) And what happens? I break down and cry . . . I'm sorry, Misha! Hopeless, hopeless! I'm sorry! (*His head sinks into his hands.*)

> Enter GLAGOLYEV *through the open door, leaning heavily on a stick, breathing with difficulty.*

GLAGOLYEV. Platonov?

> PLATONOV *lifts his head out of his hands and gazes blankly at* GLAGOLYEV.

Forgive me . . . (*To* VOYNITZEV:) Sergey Pavlovich . . . (*To* PLATONOV:) Look, this is very awkward . . . (*He glances at* VOYNITZEV.) Very awkward indeed. But I must know! And I must know today! My whole future depends upon your answer . . . Sit down, if I may . . . Walked here . . . Not as well as I might be . . . (*He sits down on the sofa.*) Yes, well . . . You know, of course, that I have long cherished certain hopes with regard to Anna Petrovna . . . In the last few days, however, I have been told certain things by certain people . . . They may be lying, of course . . . It may be mere rumour . . . But they say that Anna Petrovna . . . Or rather they say that you . . . Or let me put it like this: I have, as you know, a great respect for women, but . . . Have pity on me, Platonov . . . !

PLATONOV. I know only one thing, my friend.

GLAGOLYEV. Yes?

PLATONOV. I know that there is nothing but corruption under the sun.

> PLATONOV *picks up the revolver and goes out.*

GLAGOLYEV (*to* VOYNITZEV). Is this true?

VOYNITZEV (*lifts his head and registers* GLAGOLYEV's *presence for the first time*). What?

GLAGOLYEV. I realise how painful this is for you. But I must know! Has she — have they — do you know of any circumstance that might unfit her to be a wife?

VOYNITZEV *weeps.*

I see. I see. Thank you for your frankness. So much for love, then. So much for respect.

Enter ANNA PETROVNA *through the open door.*

ANNA PETROVNA. Misha! I can't find him . . . Oh, you're *here!* What are you doing here?

GLAGOLYEV. I have been taking a lesson from the schoolmaster. And now I am going forth into the world to put that lesson into practice. I'm going to start living before I die! One thing I shall never do, though. I shall never foul my own nest! I'll do my living in someone else's backyard!

ANNA PETROVNA. I thought you were going to catch the evening train?

GLAGOLYEV. I *am* going to catch the evening train! To Paris!

Exit GLAGOLYEV, *slamming the door behind him.*

ANNA PETROVNA. To Paris . . . ? Sergey, we've lost the estate! What's happened? What are you doing here? What have you been telling him?

VOYNITZEV. Nothing. He was talking to Platonov.

ANNA PETROVNA. Platonov? And Platonov told him . . . ? What did Platonov tell him?

VOYNITZEV. I wasn't listening.

ANNA PETROVNA. You weren't listening? You just sat there and did nothing while they took the estate away from you? God gave this estate to your ancestors! Now people walk in and take it away from you again — and you don't even ask them why!

VOYNITZEV. I don't care about the estate.

ANNA PETROVNA. Sergey! Where are we going to go? What are we going to eat? We're finished!

VOYNITZEV. I've lost something infinitely more precious to me than the estate. I've lost my wife.

ANNA PETROVNA. What do you mean, you've lost your wife? She was alive and well half-an-hour ago — I saw her!

VOYNITZEV. She's in love with someone else.

ANNA PETROVNA. Don't be silly. Concentrate on the estate . . . How *could* she be in love with someone else? There's no one in this miserable little place to be in love with! There's only the doctor. She's not in love with the doctor! There are only a few elderly landowners and a retired colonel and . . . Oh, no!

VOYNITZEV. Yes.

ANNA PETROVNA. No, no! That's not possible! I can tell you that for a fact!

VOYNITZEV. She's his mistress. She told me herself.

ANNA PETROVNA. Oh no. Oh no . . . (*She sits down.*) But what could he possibly see in her? And what were *you* doing, pray? You're supposed to be her husband! Have you no eyes in your head? You just sit there snivelling while they take the world away all round you! What sort of man are you? Anyway, Platonov isn't in love with her. He's seduced her, that's all. He doesn't love her, I can assure you of that! In fact I see now what he's running away from . . . He's leaving tonight. Did you know that?

VOYNITZEV. They're leaving together.

ANNA PETROVNA. Nonsense! Sofya's at home! I saw her!

The door is flung open. SOFYA *stands on the threshold, with a suitcase, hatboxes, ulsters, etc.*

SOFYA (*bitterly*). Your word of honour, Platonov! You gave me your word of honour!

She comes face to face with ANNA PETROVNA *and* VOYNITZEV. *Pause.*

ANNA PETROVNA. What fools men are! A flutter of the eye-lashes, and their back's broken! I'm sorry, Sergey.

VOYNITZEV. I'm going to shoot myself.

SOFYA (*quietly*). Where is he?

VOYNITZEV. Where's my revolver?

ANNA PETROVNA. What could he begin to see in a little ninny like you? I'm sorry, but that's what you are — an insipid little ninny!

SOFYA. Where is he?

ANNA PETROVNA. And now you've lost him again!

VOYNITZEV. I've lost my revolver.

ANNA PETROVNA. Your revolver?

VOYNITZEV. I put it on the table.

ANNA PETROVNA. Your estate — your wife — your revolver . . . ! Can't you keep your hands on anything?

VOYNITZEV. He must have picked it up, and . . .

SOFYA (*urgently*). Where is he?

A shot, off.

ANNA PETROVNA (*to* VOYNITZEV). You've killed him.

SOFYA (*to* VOYNITZEV). You gave him your revolver.

ANNA PETROVNA. You put it on the table in front of him.

SOFYA. You watched him pick it up.

VOYNITZEV. No!

ANNA PETROVNA. Then you cold-bloodedly sat here.

VOYNITZEV. No!

SOFYA. And waited.

VOYNITZEV. No! No!

ANNA PETROVNA. And kept us talking until . . .

Enter PLATONOV. *He crosses in silence to the table and puts the revolver back on it.*

PLATONOV. They've shot him.

ANNA PETROVNA. Platonov!

SOFYA. Are you all right?

PLATONOV. It was the peasants. They've shot him!

TWO PEASANTS *approach the window, dragging something out of sight.*

FIRST PEASANT. Sitting on a tree-stump, he was.

SECOND PEASANT. Gazing at the old schoolhouse.

FIRST PEASANT. Didn't run. Didn't move.

SECOND PEASANT. Reckon he'd gone a bit soft in the head.

FIRST PEASANT. Want to see him?

They haul the dead OSIP *up above the level of the window-ledge by his hair.*

ANNA PETROVNA. Osip!

SOFYA. Horrible! Horrible!

VOYNITZEV. Take him away!

The TWO PEASANTS *drop* OSIP *out of sight.*

SECOND PEASANT. An eye for an eye, and a head for a horse!

Laughing, they drag the body away. PLATONOV *pours himself vodka.*

ANNA PETROVNA. Poor Osip! He used to bring me baby birds. He tried to kiss me once.

SOFYA (*to* PLATONOV). That could have been you, lying dead out there.

PLATONOV *drinks.*

VOYNITZEV. If he were half a man, it would be.

ANNA PETROVNA. Yes, now listen, Platonov . . .

SOFYA. It's after eight! You gave me your word of honour!

PLATONOV (*holds up his hand*). I haven't come back to listen to reproaches. I've come back because I discovered something important while I was standing out there with the gun in my hand. I looked at Osip lying there in his blood and I knew for certain: I don't want to die! I looked death in the face; and I chose life! I know you're all unhappy. But what about me? I've lost everything! My honour — my home — my loved ones! I know you're all suffering torments. But think of me, standing out there with the gun in my hand, agonising between life and death! I come back to you hoping to be understood — I throw myself on your mercy — and what happens? You attack me like wild animals! All right — I apologise! I beg your forgiveness! What more do you want of me? Wasn't that one accursed night and all its consequences enough for you? My arm hurts — I'm as hungry as a starving dog — I'm cold — I'm ill — I'm shaking with fever . . . I'm going to lie down. (*He lies down on the sofa.*) I'm not going out again. It's raining out there.

    Pause. They all gaze at him.

SOFYA. Why are we standing here?

ANNA PETROVNA. Yes, are we bewitched?

VOYNITZEV. Platonov, are you running away or aren't you?

ANNA PETROVNA. And if so with whom?

    Enter COLONEL TRILETZKY.

COLONEL TRILETZKY. She's taken poison! She's swallowed the matches!

PLATONOV (*sits up*). Sasha?

SOFYA. Oh, no!

ANNA PETROVNA. She's not . . . ?

COLONEL TRILETZKY. She would be, if her brother hadn't found her. He's trying to save her. Mishenka, I beg you — go to her! Never mind what's happened. Just go to her and tell her you love her! Comfort her, Misha! Help us to save her!

PLATONOV (*tries to get up and fails*). Can't stand. Can't get my balance.

COLONEL TRILETZKY. Misha! Please!

PLATONOV. I'm ill, too, Father-in-law! I'm a sick man! I'm on fire! Water! Give me some water!

COLONEL TRILETZKY *hands him a jug.* PLATONOV *drinks straight from it.*

ANNA PETROVNA. He's drunk. I'll go.

SOFYA. *I'll* go.

ANNA PETROVNA. You?

SOFYA. I'll beg her to forgive me!

Exit SOFYA.

ANNA PETROVNA. Sofya! Come back!

Exit ANNA PETROVNA *after* SOFYA.

VOYNITZEV. Anna Petrovna! Sofya! Both of you! Don't make things any worse . . . !

Exit VOYNITZEV *after* ANNA PETROVNA.

COLONEL TRILETZKY. My only daughter, Misha!

PLATONOV. I'm a swine! I'm such a swine!

COLONEL TRILETZKY. My little girl, Misha!

PLATONOV. But, my God, I've been punished for it! Well and truly punished! Knocked down and run over, like a dog in the street.

COLONEL TRILETZKY. Don't keep her waiting, Misha!

PLATONOV. I can scarcely hold my head up on my shoulders! Look, it's going to fall off!

COLONEL TRILETZKY. It's nothing, Misha. You've been drinking that's all.

PLATONOV. No, I've got a fever. I've been out in the rain.

COLONEL TRILETZKY. It's not raining, Misha.

PLATONOV. Are you my father-in-law? Or are you my father? I can't think.

COLONEL TRILETZKY. Sasha's father! Poor little Sasha! She's sinking, Misha!

PLATONOV. Sasha's father! Are you? I can't see you. All I can see is little soldiers. Little green and yellow soldiers in pointed caps. They're crawling over everything . . . ! I need a doctor! Get me a doctor!

Enter GREKOVA *through the open door.*

COLONEL TRILETZKY. Wait there, Misha. I'll tell Kolya. (*To* GREKOVA.) Look after him. He's ill. And Sasha's ill. (*To* PLATONOV.) I'll see if Kolya can leave Sasha for a moment . . .

Exit COLONEL TRILETZKY.

PLATONOV (*flaps his hand in front of his eyes*). All these flies everywhere! Clouds of flies! I can't see anything! Shoot the flies . . . (*He picks up the revolver.*)

GREKOVA. No! No! Please! (*She tries to take the revolver.*)

PLATONOV (*points the revolver at her*). Who's this?

GREKOVA. It's me!

PLATONOV. The doctor, is it?

GREKOVA. Marya Yefimovna!

PLATONOV. Can't see you. Flies everywhere.

GREKOVA. Beetle-juice!

PLATONOV. Beetle-juice? My mortal enemy! (*He points the revolver.*)

GREKOVA. No! No! I got your message!

PLATONOV. Message?

GREKOVA. I met him at the ford — I had the pony and trap — I've galloped all the way . . . I just want to say, don't! Please don't!!

PLATONOV. Don't what?

GREKOVA. You said you were . . . going away. Going away forever. I knew at once. Please don't! (*She holds out her hand for the revolver.*) Please give it to me!

PLATONOV. I'm ill. I've got a fever.

GREKOVA. I'll look after you.

PLATONOV. Got to have water.

GREKOVA. I'll give you water. (*She picks up the jug.*) If you give me that.

PLATONOV. Water . . . water . . . (*He exchanges the revolver for the jug, and drinks.*)

GREKOVA. Thank God I got here in time!

PLATONOV. I can't stay here. I've got to get to bed.

GREKOVA. I'll put you to bed in my house. I've got the trap outside.

PLATONOV. Quickly! Quickly! Help me!

> GREKOVA *puts the revolver down, safely out of his reach, and goes to him.*

Hand! Give me your hand . . . ! Oh, cold hand! Lovely hand! Kiss your lovely cold hand . . .

GREKOVA. No, no . . .

PLATONOV. And your lovely cold cheek . . . (*He pulls her down into his lap and kisses her cheek.*)

GREKOVA. You mustn't do that.

PLATONOV. I'm not going to seduce you, my dear! No fit state at the moment. Can't even see you properly . . . Can't see you, but I love you all the same. Love everyone. Never wanted to upset anyone. And what happens? I upset everyone! (*He kisses her hands.*)

GREKOVA. I know what happened. It was Sofya, wasn't it.

PLATONOV. Sofya, Zizi, Mimi, Masha . . . There are so many of you! And I'm in love with you all! I love everyone — and everyone loves me. I insult them, I treat them abominably — and they love me just the same! (*He puts his arm round her.*) Take that Beetle-juice girl, for example. I indecently assaulted her — I kissed her . . . (*He kisses her.*) . . . and she's still in love with me . . . Oh, you are Beetle-juice, aren't you. Sorry.

GREKOVA. You're all muddled up inside that head of yours.

She embraces him. He flinches.

You're in pain, too. Tell me where it hurts.

PLATONOV. In Platonov — that's where it hurts . . . *Are* you in love with me, then? Are you really?

GREKOVA. Yes. (*She kisses him.*) I am in love with you.

PLATONOV. Yes, they're all in love with me. Once I used to moralise away to them all, and they loved me for it. Now I seduce them instead, and they still love me.

GREKOVA. You do what you like with me. I don't mind. (*She weeps.*) You're only human, after all. And that's enough for me.

Enter DR TRILETZKY.

DR TRILETZKY (*cheerfully*). Misha! We've got a surprise for you! (*He freezes at the sight of* GREKOVA *sitting in* PLATONOV's *lap.*)

Enter SASHA, *supported by* ANNA PETROVNA *and* SOFYA, *and followed by* VOYNITZEV *and* COLONEL TRILETZKY.

ANNA PETROVNA (*to* SASHA). Come on, my dear. You know you want to see him.

SOFYA (*to* SASHA). You know *he* wants to see *you* . . .

The women halt at the spectacle before them.

VOYNITZEV. Terrible tragedy!

COLONEL TRILETZKY. But it's got a happy ending.

> VOYNITZEV *and* COLONEL TRILETZKY *halt in their turn.* GREKOVA *hides her face in* PLATONOV*'s neck.* PLATONOV *hugs her, unaware of his audience.*

PLATONOV. No fit state now. Never you fear, though — when I get better again I'll seduce you like the rest of them.

> DR TRILETZKY *is the first to move.*

DR TRILETZKY. Misha! If I've told you once I've told you a thousand times . . . !

SOFYA. The revolver! Where's the revolver? (*She finds it and points it at* PLATONOV.)

GREKOVA (*jumps up and interposes herself between* SOFYA *and* PLATONOV). No! No!

VOYNITZEV. Sofya! It was all going to be all right!

ANNA PETROVNA (*tries to take the revolver from* SOFYA). Give me that! I'll do it myself!

GREKOVA. I love him!

SASHA (*left unsupported, sinks to her knees*). Kill me! Not him!

COLONEL TRILETZKY (*vacillates uncertainly between* SASHA *and the others*). Sasha . . . ! Sofya Yegorovna . . . !

DR TRILETZKY. Misha!

VOYNITZEV. Sofya!

COLONEL TRILETZKY. Kolya . . . ! Sasha . . . !

GREKOVA. We love each other!

SOFYA (*in a terrible voice*). Stand back! All of you!

> *Enter* MARKO *through the open door.*

PLATONOV. Wait! What does *he* want?

> *They all turn and see* MARKO.

MARKO. Three rubles, if you're happy, sir.

PLATONOV. Happy? My cup runneth over! Give him four!

In the instant while they automatically look around for four rubles, PLATONOV *jumps out of the window.*

SOFYA *and the others rush to the window after him. As they do so there is the sound of an approaching train whistle, and they all turn, struck by the same thought. They run out of the door; and the world falls apart. Amidst the gathering roar of the train the rear wall of the house moves aside and the lights go down. The forest and the railway line of the previous scene are revealed beyond. Stumbling towards us between the rails is* PLATONOV. *He stops, blinded by the brilliant headlight of a train approaching from behind the heads of the audience, its whistle screaming. He staggers back a step or two, trying to wave the train away like the flies. Then sudden blackness, and the great roar of the train, its note falling as it passes us. The red tail light of the train appears at the front of the stage and dwindles rapidly into the smoke left by the locomotive. There is a smell of sulphur in the air.*

Blackout.